KEYWORDS OF FAITH

First published in 1992 by
SAINT ANDREW PRESS
121 George Street, Edinburgh EH2 4YN

Copyright 1992 © James A Simpson, Angus T Stewart,
Alan A S Reid

ISBN 0 7152 0653 2

British Library Cataloguing in Publication Data
  Keywords of faith.
    I. Simpson, James A., *1934-*
    II. Stewart, Angus T. III. Reid, Alan A. S.
    827.914080382

  ISBN 0-7152-0653-2

This book has been set in 11/12.5 pt Times Roman.

The Publisher would like to acknowledge *Life and Work* for allow-
ing the use in this book of material which originally appeared as
articles in the aforementioned magazine.

The Publisher would also like to acknowledge financial assistance
from *The Drummond Trust* towards publication of this volume.

Printed and bound by Bell and Bain Ltd., Glasgow

Contents

Part II TWIN WORDS

Introduction

THE Gospel has many social and political implications; but if, in concentrating on these, the Church neglects the great spiritual themes, she will cease to minister to people's deeper hungers. The Church has something to say which no one else can say—and it is not primarily moral exhortations, or political or economic judgments on society, but an understanding of God and the nature and destiny of humanity. The Church is called to speak plainly about these things: 'to unscrew the inscrutable,' as the black preacher said.

C S Lewis once suggested that before ordination was permitted, a minister should first have to pass an examination in translating the scholarly, technical language of theology into the language of the kitchen and the shop floor: 'Any fool can write learned language. The vernacular is the real test.'

Like C S Lewis, Professor William Barclay rendered the Church invaluable service by doing just that: interpreting for the people in the pew and for his huge television audiences what the biblical scholars and theologians were saying. William Barclay attributed any success he had in communicating with ordinary folk to an old woman who lived alone in a single-end in Renfrew where he ministered for several years. When she took ill he visited her regularly. Once, after the manner and privilege of old ladies, she said, 'When you have been here talking to me, and sometimes putting up a wee prayer, it has been grand, and I have understood every word you have said. But when you're in yon pulpit on the Sunday, you're awa' o'er ma heid!' That timely criticism prompted Barclay to simplify his style of teaching, preaching and writing.

During the past century the Church has spent a great deal of time and effort translating the Bible into foreign languages like Swahili, Urdu and Chinamwanga. Nowadays the great need is to translate 'the language of Zion' into the vernacular; to reinterpret the biblical themes of *grace, repentance, incarnation* and *atonement* in the thought-forms and language of our day, in terms meaningful to our unchurched friends. For although these old words once spoke with meaning and power, today many of the key words are considerably devalued; they have been heard so often that people don't really listen any more.

Whereas some words have a reasonably fixed value, especially those which refer to objects we can handle—like a chair, a pen, a daffodil, a shoe—this is not so with words which describe intangible things. *Justice, truth, freedom, love* mean different things to different people.

To a communist, *freedom* means one thing; to a rebellious teenager it means quite another. And in the New Testament it means something quite different still.

In Iraq and Iran *justice* means something very different from what it means in Britain.

Love for many of our contemporaries is equated with the desire for emotional and sexual satisfaction with another person; whereas love as Mother Teresa understands it—and as Jesus understood it—is a costly, caring, sacrificial concern for others.

There is no such thing as timeless English. Words, especially religious words, words that have to do with the depth of things, get tired and stale the way other words do, and the way people do. Sometimes they have picked up such unhelpful associations and resonances that they have to be replaced or, at very least, reinterpreted in such a way that they will be heard as new. T S Eliot reminds us in his poem 'Four Quartets' that:

Words strain,
Crack and sometimes break, under the burden,
Under the tension, slip, slide, perish,
Decay with imprecision, will not stay in place,
Will not stay still ...
Last year's words belong to last year's language,
And this year's words demand another voice.

Anyone can say, 'Believe in the Lord Jesus Christ and be saved.' But can we say this in such a way that unchurched friends will understand what we are talking about? It is easier to remain orthodox by keeping to the old words and phrases such as *conversion, salvation, born again* and *open your life to Christ,* than it is to make the time or effort to dig down into their biblical meaning and express their enduring truth in contemporary terms. The person who tries to remint the old words, to restate their meaning in as fresh a way as possible, will always be skirting *the edge of heresy.* But only those who run this risk will communicate effectively. The writers of this book believe that part of the ongoing task of the Church is to speak of the 'faith once delivered' in contemporary terms. We feel obliged not to say different things from our forebears, but to say things *differently*.

A popular hymn speaks of Jesus as '*Prophet, priest* and *king.*' Unfortunately for many today, all three words have lost their original power and significance. Today many think of a *prophet* not as the Old Testament writers did—as a man with the wisdom of God on his lips—but rather as one who foretells the future. Many think of a *priest* not as one who bridges the gulf between God and man, but as one who wears coloured vestments and officiates at mass. Even the word *king* could mislead, for Christ's was a unique kind of kingly authority. His royal robe was a towel and his sceptre was a basin.

It would be naive to think that once people better understand the Christian faith, they will accept it and live in the light of it. But at least people should have a clear understanding of what they are accepting or rejecting. In Acts we read of Paul's defence before the Jewish Council: 'When they heard him speaking to them in Hebrew, they became even quieter.' At least to begin with they gave him a hearing because they could understand him.

Up until the 1950s theology was mainly written by people who were involved regularly in preaching and pastoral work, but in more recent years theological books have been written increasingly by professors working often in predominantly secular universities. Whereas earlier this century theology was for the most part written for the Church, today it is increasingly written for the academic community. Though such theology may thrive for a time in the rarefied atmosphere of a divinity faculty, unless it is considerably simplified and clarified it will have little or no impact on the worshipping congregation. With this in mind I approached two friends, Alan Reid and Angus Stewart, both able communicators, to help me write a book that might be of help not only to those in the pew who are often more than a little confused as to what to believe, but also to the many unchurched folk who secretly would like to believe.

Inevitably in trying to simplify Christian belief one runs the risk of giving superficial answers to hard questions and compromising the dimension of depth and mystery that there is to faith and life. I hope we have avoided both pitfalls.

James A Simpson

Part I

THE ABC OF FAITH

NO attempt has been made in this abbreviated alphabet of Christianity to define all the keywords of faith. Readers will immediately think of many which they feel should have been included—like *gospel, vocation, peace, reconciliation, righteousness*—but to have included these and many other keywords would have required a much larger volume: in fact, nothing short of a dictionary of the Christian faith. That not being possible within the compass of a modestly priced book, selection was necessary.

We make no definitive claims for what we have written. But it is our hope that these brief chapters will help some of our readers reach a clearer understanding of some of the central beliefs of the Christian faith.

Almighty

A MANAGING director had the habit of bawling at his employees when things went wrong, or when he wanted something done in a hurry. He moved them, like pawns on a chess board, from office to office, and town to town, with no consideration for their family life. An employee once said of him, 'He thinks he is Lord God *Almighty*.'

That is a slander on the character of God. An *almighty* monarch or dictator might behave in this way, but not an *almighty* father. Jesus prayed, 'Father all things are possible to you.' He did not pray, 'Almighty dictator, all things are possible.' He said 'father.' God's power is severely limited by his fatherhood.

A former Dean of St Paul's, London, tells how as a boy he suddenly lost faith in God. 'If God can prevent evil and does not, he is not benevolent; and if God would prevent evil but cannot, he is not almighty.' The Dean realised later that the problem arose from a misunderstanding of the word *almighty*. He had mentally assumed that *almighty* meant 'able to do everything.' He did not realise that it is only defective and capricious characters like Saddam Hussein or Adolf Hitler who are '*capable of doing anything*'!

A man who, during the Second World War, had close personal contact with Eichmann, tells how he once, in the presence of Eichmann, made reference to God. Eichmann mockingly laughed and said, 'Do you really believe in God?' When the Czech replied that he did, Eichmann asked, 'Is your God more powerful than I am? Behind that door are 500 Jews. In five minutes I could release them all or kill them all. Is your God more powerful than that?' It was an impossible question to answer, for the nature

of divine power is so radically different from power as
Eichmann conceived it. God's power is always motivated
and used in the service of love, never in the service of hate
and prejudice. God will not act contrary to his purpose as
a loving father. If this is impotence, then God in this sense
is powerless.

I suppose God could have made us all puppets. Jerked
by divine strings we would unhesitatingly have carried
out his wishes. But in giving us free-will—freedom of
choice —he had to take the risk that we might choose not
to co-operate.

In a wonderful book entitled *The Splendour of God,*
the story is told of Adoniram Judson and his wife Anne.
It is a story of hardship, suffering, disappointment, peril
and death. It is a sad story, yet it thrills you from first page
to last. Though the Judsons were highly respected, they
had few converts. The children born to them soon died.
Judson's wife Anne soon followed them to the grave. Though
he was imprisoned later in awful surroundings, treated
harshly, chained for a year and a half to the floor with just
enough food to keep his broken body going, Judson never
became embittered. He never stopped caring for those who
ill-treated him. Because there was seen in this human life
love akin to the divine, love that was undying, that refused
to give up, the author chose as his title for Judson's story,
The Splendour of God. Had I written the book, I would
have been tempted to add one more word, *The Splendour
of Almighty God.*

It was Christianity which introduced the world to the
idea of a God of immense power who suffers, a God who
exercises his sovereignty more through crosses than thrones.
What pain and heartbreak God must know as he contem-
plates what his children still do with the freedom he has
given them. One thinks of the horror of Belsen, Tianaman
Square and Kuwait—of the savage confusion of Northern

Ireland—of the crimes and violence in our cities. Though it must often break God's heart, he refuses to make people good against their wishes. He has to let his prodigal sons go their own way. He goes on appealing and seeking to persuade them that there is a better way, but refuses to compel. He refuses to make them slaves who only obey because they have to, or puppets who cannot but respond. He is a God who patiently waits for our consent.

Sometimes such incredible patience has been understood as divine indifference. The Psalmist cried:

Keep not thou silence, O God
Hold not thy peace, and be not still O God
For lo thine enemies make a tumult. (83:2)

When wickedness spills over and hurts the innocent and those we love, when dishonesty seems to prosper and virtue goes to the wall, we are tempted to cry with Thomas Carlyle, 'Why does God sit in his heaven and do nothing?' We know what we would do. If we had even a small part of God's power, we would call on people everywhere in tones of thunder to change their ways or else! 'If I were God and the world had treated me as it has treated him,' said Martin Luther, 'I would kick the wretched thing to pieces.' An almighty ruler might, but not an *almighty father.*

Instead God waits with infinite patience for us to grow up, for our little minds to catch up with his. Dictators may bull-doze people, violate the human will and thus quickly achieve their little ends, but in the long time purposes of God, the Almighty Father must wait for our willing co-operation.

'Let there be light, and there was light.' Whereas for God, Creation was relatively easy, there being no resistance or disobedience, redemption is infinitely difficult. Yet it is in redemption that God's power is most clearly seen,

in the divine love which alone can change the human heart
and align our wills to his. The New Testament records the
awesome cost of redemption to God. There we hear a baby
crying in a manger—a young itinerant preacher patiently
trying to persuade people to follow him, to care as he cares
—and finally a voice that says through lips swollen with
agony: 'Father forgive them.'

> *What humbles me to the dust and*
> *Bows down my soul with awe and adoration,*
> *Is that the mighty God, in whose hands*
> *Is all the power in heaven and earth,*
> *Who might if he were less great,*
> *By overwhelming will*
> *Break down my will,*
> *Comes rather to my heart's door, and*
> *Stoops there to knock.*

Atonement

THE word *atonement* can be simply explained as '*at-one-ment*' because it refers to a making at one of individuals or parties who have fallen out or disagreed.

On my desk as I write this there are three small lumps of concrete. They are fragments of the Berlin Wall which were brought back to Scotland by a young woman who was visiting Berlin recently. The dramatic events which led to the demolition of the Berlin Wall and the breaking down of the separation between East and West Germany provide an example of *atonement*: making at one peoples formerly divided. It has an echo in the New Testament where Jews and Gentiles who were bitter enemies were made at one through Jesus Christ—'With his own body Jesus broke down the wall that separated them and kept them enemies' (Ephesians 2:14, GOOD NEWS BIBLE).

However, the significance of atonement does not lie in that, but in the primary reconciliation that 'God made us his friends.' The most significant barrier is the barrier between God and man: the barrier which, the Bible tells us, sin creates. Isaiah said long ago, 'It is your sins that separate you from God,' and the idea that sin creates a barrier goes right back to the story of the garden of Eden. No matter how you understand that story, there is deep significance in the ancient writer's insight: when Adam and Eve 'heard the Lord God walking in the garden, they hid from him among the trees' (Genesis 3:8, GNB). By the eating of the forbidden fruit, a barrier had been erected, breaking the close fellowship with which the story began. Only when that barrier is removed can the other barriers be dismantled and the New Testament thrust is that in the Cross of Christ this is what happened.

A key verse is Romans 4:25—'Because of our sins he was handed over to die, and he was raised to life in order to put us right with God.' But that Good News Bible translation does less than justice to the Greek text. Although it rightly shows that our sins were the reason for Jesus' death, it fails to show what an identical phrase in Greek means, that our being put right with God was *the reason for Christ being raised to life*. In other words, instead of thinking of Christ's resurrection as the *cause* of our being put right with God, the resurrection is the *result* of the atonement being completed. Sin was the reason for Jesus' death, and the atonement the reason for his resurrection.

There are many pictures which try to explain something of the immensity of the Cross. From Leviticus 16 we get the strange story of the scapegoat which in some way carried the sins of the people out into the desert. We have the New Testament concept of 'the ransom', and we have the picture of Jesus 'bearing our sins upon the Cross.' None of these pictures conveys all of the truth, but they all point at something which is basic to each of them: namely that in the Cross, God removed the barrier which had separated people from God. The Good News Bible has a splendid way of putting this: 'Our message is that God was making all mankind his friends through Christ' (2 Corinthians 5:19). In *The Sacred Diary of Adrian Plass* (Marshall Pickering), we read of a visiting preacher whose message was simply 'God is nice and he likes us.'

The idea of Jesus dying for us is one that puzzles many people. A number of years ago a friend married a Canadian girl. In those days the law was such that from the moment of her marriage she became a British citizen—in other words she entered into all that was her husband's. That is how I find it best to think of the atonement. Jesus died upon a Cross and somehow when resurrection morning came, sin had been dealt with. We benefit from that atonement, we become forgiven, we enter into new life in virtue of our relationship with Jesus. It is this living relationship which makes the atonement real for us in our experience.

Once the barrier between God and us has been removed, then we can begin to see the barriers that separate us from each other being dismantled; and the Berlin Wall becomes not only a symbol of European unity, but also a picture of the prospect that 'man to man the world o'er shall brothers be for a' that.'

Blessing

'BLESS you,' she said, not looking up from her ironing. The sound of his sneeze filled the room. He looked at her with mild irritation over his handkerchief, wondering why she always said the same thing, automatically, without wondering whether it meant anything. Probably it was because her mother had done exactly the same thing. Anyway, it wasn't worth having a row about.

But what a strange thing it was to say. For a moment—at the ironing board—she became a priest. To *bless* someone was a religious function, wasn't it? It was to put the goodness of God upon another in some way. Perhaps when you sneezed you were, for a millisecond, very near death—was that it? And when someone *blessed* you (however thoughtlessly), were you in that instant a little nearer God than you were before? He thought of the number of times he had, a little self-consciously, signed off his phone calls to his daughter with the phrase 'God bless.' It was a phrase you used to signal that your love and care wouldn't stop when the phone call ended. He decided that he would do some research on the word tomorrow ….

He discovered that the verb *to bless* is one of the great foundation words of the Bible. It is a characteristic, unique and special activity of God in Creation ('And God blessed them, and said, be fruitful … '—'And God blessed the seventh day …'). God does not only create, with marvellous fecundity and specificity. Having created, and looked with a craftsman's joy at his creation (if one may put it so), it is as if he puts his hands very lovingly over each created thing and says a prayer, 'Be fruitful.' 'Be healthy and very happy, and rejoice in what you are.' The blessing is terribly

14

important—a fragile, lovely expression of a hope. And once said, it is said. The future of that created thing is charged with the blessing, pregnant with it, and the blessing cannot be taken back.

Later in the Bible it becomes clear that this very special function of blessing or consecrating is exercised by certain individuals, in God's name, in a derivative way. Heads of families have a sacred duty to bless their children. The great spiritual 'classic' here is the Jacob-Esau narrative, when Jacob—although the younger son—cheats his elder brother out of his father's blessing. This blessing is not just a general parental expression of goodwill, such as any parent might use in saying goodnight to their child. It is a sacred transference of God's good hope from father to eldest son, once and for all, irrevocably given. In the deep and terrible psychological resolution of the Jacob story, a moment of dread come-uppance is visited on the perpetrator of the deception. He wrestles, in a night vision, with an unknown stranger (God? his father? Esau? an angel? his own better self?) and hears himself shouting into the early dawn, 'I will not let you go unless you bless me!' The blessing of God is something one has to take seriously—it has consequences.

You don't get much further in the Old Testament when you begin to realise that the function of blessing—'blessing the people from God'—is assigned to a specific person and his descendants. Moses' brother Aaron becomes a specially chosen instrument in God's purpose. He is to be the blesser, in God's Name, of the whole people. And his sons will all be set apart with this special function. When we baptise a baby today, we say, or sing, the great blessing that Aaron first said over the people of Israel: 'The Lord bless you and keep you. The Lord make his face to shine upon you, and be gracious unto you. The Lord lift up his countenance upon you, and give you peace.' For three

thousand years the beauty and spirituality of those words
have remained undiminished.

It becomes clear also that *blessing* is no automatic
transaction, operating independently of our will in the
matter. The great General of the Exodus, Aaron's brother
Moses, confronted the people with a choice at the end of
his life: 'Behold, I have set before you this day blessing
and cursing ....' There is a matter of a crucial choice to
be made, in our allegiances and our loyalties. The other
point to be made is that blessing is not just given to certain
individuals, specially chosen. All kinds of things are
blessed: land, work, households, children, the congregation. But as the Children of Israel shaped themselves
under God's hand through their history, it became clear
to them—through those with special insight into how
God works—that there would come a single figure one
day who would be specially blessed, uniquely chosen to
carry the blessing.

The central Christian perception is that Jesus Christ
is that figure. The writer to the Ephesians says that in Christ,
God has bestowed on us 'every spiritual blessing in the
heavenly realms.' Jesus revolutionised the contemporary
teaching on happiness with his famous nine sentences
(called 'The Beatitudes'), showing the kind of people
whom God really counts 'blessed.' They were not the rich,
the successful, the invulnerable, the victorious in war,
the satisfied with good things. They were the poor, the
bereaved, the hungry, the peace-makers, the people who
were driven on to God and thus knew their need of him
and their own inadequacy. To know this, said Jesus, was
to be 'truly happy', to be *blessed*. So we have, in the teaching
of Jesus, the fundamental suggestion being made that to
be *blessed* is not equivalent to being confirmed in ease,
plenty, immunity, and comfort.

Jesus, on the night before he died, said three blessings.

He blessed a cup and a piece of bread, and he set them apart forever as signs of his blood and his body, given for us all. He also blessed his disciples, and 'consecrated' them in the truth for all that was coming, so that they never forgot that he had prayed for them, individually and collectively. And the Christian Church—in every culture and language—has tried to continue his practice, in the sacrament of the Lord's Supper, and in the minister's (or priest's) responsibility 'to bless this people from God.'

A blessing is not a guarantee of immunity against danger or trouble. It is not an insurance certificate. It is a quite deliberate placing of a person or a group of people under the care of God and into the purpose of God for them. Because God wills all his children's good, we pray that this will mean health, joy, peace and true development for them. But the Christian understands each of these words very differently from the agnostic. To say this is not to be perverse or masochistic. It is to recognise, in Jesus' works, that the road to life has a narrow gate to it.

He felt a sneeze coming on, and tried to suppress it. But no, it would not be denied. 'Bless you,' she said, without looking up.

Christian

THE word *Christian* occurs only three times in the New Testament and yet it is one of the most commonly used words today. We use it in different senses—we speak of a *Christian* country, of a *Christian* act, or we say of ourselves, 'I'm not much of a *Christian*.'

The meaning of the word in the first century can help us to understand what it ought to mean today. The word referred to people with certain distinctive features. The first feature perhaps was that they were people with a Master. The word *Christian* was a nick-name, and yet the root (meaning 'Christ-people') was serious enough because it means 'those who belong to Christ.' However we care to translate the word in the New Testament, it certainly has this dimension to it. Perhaps a useful analogy is that of 'Christening,' where the name of Christ is said over a child. In much the same way, when we accept the name *Christian*, we are being enrolled on the side of Jesus, for it speaks of a personal relationship. It takes us back to the very beginnings of the Church, for we are told in Acts 2:14, 'They realised that they had been companions of Jesus.' This is the basic meaning of the word *Christian*.

But there is a second meaning: Christians are people with a message. In Antioch where the name was first given, there was plenty of wealth, plenty of religious worship, and plenty of loose living. To this town the Christians came with a message, which was simply 'the good news about the Lord Jesus,' and that was distinctive. The word *Christian* today ought to signify a beacon of light in a darkened world—a signal of hope in an atmosphere of despair.

When the Christians were first called by that name in

Antioch, there is an interesting word used in the text. The word *called* means 'transacted business': it means in effect 'they transacted business under the name of Christian.' The significance of this is that the distinctive thing about them was not their missionary work or their preaching, but their living. It was the way these people lived that marked them out as different. There is a need to grasp this today because quite often we get to fever pitch over the whole question of evangelism and outreach from the Church, whereas the New Testament emphasis seems to be a much steadier one of the witness of a Christian life. It is not a coincidence that the man who gave Antioch such a boost was Barnabas, who in the New Testament spent his whole time encouraging and supporting other people. It is this kind of behaviour that earns a person the right to be called *Christian*.

The Church

THE Greek word for *Church* is *ekklesia*, from which we derive our word 'ecclesiastical.' That is the word which those who translated the Hebrew Bible into Greek used for the 'congregation' of Israel in the Old Testament, and it is a word with an illuminating history from classical Greek.

It means 'called out.' A herald was dispatched to summon the citizens to attend a meeting, and those who responded and turned up to the meeting were called the *ekklesia*. In using this word for the *Church*, the writers were indicating that the Church consists of those who have heard, and who have responded to, the call of Jesus: 'Follow me.'

But in today's world, we can usefully think of the meaning of the word *Church* in the following ways.

First, as a PLACE. We all know what it means to speak of 'the Church in Duke Street, or Pont Street'—we are describing a building; usually one with a tower or spire, perhaps with problems of dry rot (sometimes infecting the pulpit!), sometimes draughty, sometimes welcoming. We speak of the Church as 'God's house'—and that can be both bad and good.

I remember being at the opening of a Church building when the preacher said, 'This is God's house—come and visit him as often as you can.' To me, that was almost blasphemous, for it seemed to indicate that God stayed in that particular building and nowhere else.

But it can also be good. When our elder son was four, we were preparing to take the harvest gifts to Church for the Harvest Thanksgiving, and he said to his mother, 'We're going to God's house?' Quite delighted that he

had learned that the Church was the house of God, his
mother said yes. Then he demolished her sense of achieve-
ment by saying, 'Good—then we'll see God.'

You couldn't fault his logic: when you go to Granny's
house, you see Granny; when you go to Derek's house,
you see Derek; and so when you go to God's house, you
see … ? Of course, you could say the little lad was totally
wrong in this because nobody has ever seen God. Yet perhaps he wasn't too far from the truth. While we do not see
God in the sense in which we see uncle or aunt, brother
or sister, we can see God in other people: God revealed
himself in the person of Jesus, and God reveals himself
to us today through others, through their words, through
their actions, and through their lives. And so, we could
also say that the lad was gloriously right.

For the Church is also PEOPLE. In 1 Peter 2, there is
a lovely picture of the Church, where the writer invites
his hearers, 'Come as living stones, and let yourselves be
used in building the spiritual temple' (1 Peter 2:5, GNB).
The Church is people—old and young together—who
have heard the call of Jesus, even though 'faint and far
away,' and have at least begun to respond. I like the idea of
being built together with other folk into the Church. Some
years ago, in the course of reconstructing our Victorian
style garden, we removed the large stones that bordered
the flower beds. We were puzzled when we discovered
that many of them bore the marks of the mason's chisel,
and then it dawned on us that they had been intended for
the Church or Manse, but had been found unsuitable. What
a picture of Christians! There are some who are not part
of the building, and how much they are missing.

Now if we stopped there it would all be nice and cosy
—and quite untrue to the New Testament. For the Church
is also a PRESENCE. One of the Bible's favourite metaphors
for the Church is 'the body of Christ', for the Church is

the means by which Jesus continues his work in the world today. In Acts 1:1, Luke begins his second volume with the significant words, 'In my first book I wrote about all that Jesus began to do and to teach': the inference is clear, that Jesus is *continuing* to do and to teach through his body, the *Church*.

While it is true that we can echo these words—

He has no hands but our hands to do his work today;
He has no feet but our feet to lead men in his way;
He has no voice but our voice to tell men how he died;
He has no help but our help to lead them to his side

—we have to be honest with the New Testament's view of the significance of the picture of the Church as his body. When we read, for example, 1 Corinthians 12, we find Paul deducing from 'this body' metaphor that Christians ought to care for each other, to rejoice with each other, and to suffer with each other.

I still remember that when I was a little boy my mother used to run her fingers through my hair: and I can vividly recall the feeling of well-being that surged through me. Now although it was only my head that was affected, yet my whole body felt better. That is the meaning of the 'body of Christ', that Christians ought to feel for each other. Didn't Jesus give as his main command, 'Love one another'? When we do that, the love overflows to all whom we meet, and Christ is present wherever we are.

A minister known to me was having dinner with some friends. The person across the table asked him, 'How long have you been in your present church, Padre?' He answered, 'Thirteen years.' 'My God!' said the other. And the minister, without thinking, replied, 'Not quite; merely one of his representatives!' That is the calling of every Church member.

Conversion

THE word *conversion* is often an off-putting one as it is associated with a high-powered kind of religion which antagonises as many people as it attracts. Yet the word is used in the Bible, and Jesus himself used it. We can begin to approach it not by looking at its meaning in the Bible, but by thinking of its meaning in the world today.

There are two instances in which this word is common currency. The first appeared a number of years ago when homes were *converted* to North Sea gas. The second instance appeared more recently, when cars began to be *converted* from leaded to unleaded petrol. In fact, the most sophisticated exhaust device fitted to cars today is the 'catalytic *converter*'. Therefore, the word *convert,* or *conversion,* is a word that we are accustomed to.

The analogy of petrol is a very helpful one. We all know that leaded petrol is harmful to the environment we live in, that it increases the greenhouse effect we hear so much about, and that to use leaded petrol where we could be using unleaded is to be considered thoughtless about our neighbours, our children and future generations. Now, petrol is a spirit, and the spirit that drives man is equally 'environmentally unfriendly.' According to Jesus (Mark 7:21-22, GNB), this spirit is the root cause of so many evil things that corrupt and spoil the world of today and we have to realise the spirit we are using is one that is hostile to our environment.

The next stage comes when we try to change from that hurtful, harmful spirit to a spirit that will do good. The Bible calls this spirit the *Holy Spirit* or, if you prefer it, the *Spirit of Jesus*. The Spirit of Jesus is the spirit of power, love and self-control, in marked contrast to the kind of evil things that the human spirit can so often promote. Just as our cars can be changed from one form of motor spirit to another, so lives can be changed. It takes approximately 30 seconds to convert the engine of my car to unleaded fuel; for some people, conversion is sudden and dramatic, while for others it is a long, gradual process. What matters, of course, is not how long conversion takes, but which spirit provides the driving force—and this applies to our hearts, just as it applies to our cars.

This is what the New Testament calls *conversion*. It means lives changed from being controlled by the spirit of self, to being under the control of the spirit of God or the spirit of Jesus. We are given a couple of clues as to the way to find this new spirit. We are told this spirit is given to those who ask God (Luke 11:13), and also to those who obey God (Acts 5:32). It is when we ask God for his help, and begin to do what he asks of us, that we begin to realise the power of God's spirit in our lives.

Of course, that is only the beginning—it will take the rest of our lives to continue what God has begun. That is why someone neatly defined *conversion* as 'a change of heart followed by a change of direction.'

Death

THE Bible uses various pictures to describe *death*, pictures such as 'falling asleep', 'being with Christ' or 'being in Paradise.' There is one word which occurs in 2 Timothy 4:6 which gives us, as it were, a keyhole view of the Christian's concept of *death*. For those who are in union with Jesus Christ, *death* is no longer a spectre or something to be feared, but something to be regarded as a stage on the road of life. The context in which that verse is set is towards the end of Paul's life, when facing execution by the Roman sword. The Greek word used there—*analusis*—had several uses in the world of Paul's day; these uses help us to understand better what *death* means for the Christian.

First, we see death as rest. The word is used of unyoking an animal at the end of the day's work and leading it to its rest in stall or stable. This was obviously a most applicable word in the case of Paul, who had spent his life tirelessly proclaiming the Gospel and now was entitled to look forward to rest at the end of the day. I have a vivid memory of my two and a half year old son speaking about this months after his grandfather's death. He turned to me while crossing the road and simply said, 'Grandpa was tired and God just picked him up.'

But death also means release. The word *analusis* is used for setting a prisoner free from his chains. For Paul this would have a literal application, as he spent his last months in bondage under the Roman authorities. But the concept of being released is one that means a great deal to Christian people. For many of us, the time comes when life in this body becomes a life of pain and suffering, and the prospect that at the end death comes as a release is a very real and lovely one. I remember somebody who was deeply involved in the whole ministry of healing, saying to me once, 'Death is sometimes God's way of healing,' and this is abundantly true. There is a great line in a hymn which, speaking of death, says 'I'll fight life's final war with pain'—for Christians that is a precious insight.

The Greek word has two other meanings which are interesting. The first speaks of death as a return. It is in this sense that the Good News Bible translates the last verse of Psalm 23 as, 'Your house will be my home as long as I live.' The word was used by soldiers of striking camp: the time when the camps were folded up and the soldiers moved on. I well remember running a Boys' Brigade camp in Argyll and the day after the boys had gone home, looking over the campsite and seeing the yellowing patches on the ground where the tents had stood. There was no cause for grief, as the boys had gone home to sound sleep, good food and their friends. All that was left were the patches on the ground. Over Baden-Powell's grave in Africa is the simple Scout sign which means 'I have gone home.'

Another use of the word in Paul's day was by sailors. They used it to describe casting off the mooring ropes and launching out on a voyage. This is an exciting view of death as not the end of life, but in a real sense its true beginning. It is this sense that underlies Tennyson's poem 'Crossing the Bar':

> *Sunset and evening star, and one clear call for me!*
> *And may there be no moaning of the bar, when I put*
> *out to sea,*
> *But such a tide as, moving, seems asleep, too full for*
> *sound or foam,*
> *When that which drew from out the boundless deep*
> *turns again home.*
> *Twilight and evening bell, and after that the dark!*

And may there be no sadness of farewell, when I embark;
For though from out our bourne of time and place the
flood may bear me far,
I hope to see my Pilot face to face when I have crost
the bar.

Dedicated

THE word *dedicated* is widely used today. The popular press use it to describe athletes, pop singers and footballers. When used of football supporters the word usually means 'fanatical' (from which the word 'fan' is derived). And it is all too easy to think of the New Testament use of *dedication* as describing someone who is 'too heavenly minded to be of any earthly use'!

The word *dedicated* is covered some 16 times in the New Testament, where the Good News Bible uses different expressions to translate it; but to get the flavour of it, we need to look at the associated word 'holy,' which we find 72 times in the New Testament. Both words essentially refer to being 'set apart.' That is a helpful idea, as there are two senses in which someone or something can be 'set apart.'

First, it means set apart *from* any other purpose: we can think of the bread and wine used in the Communion Service, when it is 'set apart from all common uses.' Second, it means set apart *for* a special purpose: as the bread and wine are set apart to remind us of the body and blood of Jesus. But we do not use the words 'set apart' in ordinary conversation; instead, we often use the word *dedicated*. For the purpose of this article, I'd like to think of the word *dedicated* instead of the other words 'set apart' and 'holy', which tend to start us thinking along religious lines, and confine our thoughts to what happens in Church.

The word *dedicated* is one we will come across quite often today. For example, I have two *dedicated* items in my study. One is a printer, which is attached to a word processor (on which this article is being typed); and the other is a flash gun for a camera. Each is referred to by the makers as 'dedicated.' The makers of the printer and the flash gun mean that while these items *may* work with any word processor or camera, they work *best* with the ones for which they were designed. You can use them with any other make of computer or camera, but for the best results you are wise to keep to the recommended article.

This is a useful and helpful way of understanding what it means to be dedicated. Romans 1:7 in the Authorised Version speaks of Christians as 'called to be saints'; unfortunately that may convey a very pious picture of the 'unco guid', and may seem far removed from the world of today. But the Good News Bible has a splendid translation—'whom God has *called to belong to Jesus Christ.*'

There are two sides to this: the first is the positive side, for Christians are 'set apart' (dedicated) *to* Jesus. And the second is that we are 'set apart' *from* other entanglements. Like the printer and flash gun, we work best when we realise the purpose for which we were made—and this is to work with Jesus. So being dedicated does not mean being other-worldly, but simply making our relationship with Jesus our top priority. He himself spoke along these lines when he said 'without me you can do nothing' (John 15:5, GNB). And of course, if we are to be united to Jesus, then we have to be free of other entanglements: this is well put in Hebrews 12:1-2: 'Let us rid ourselves of everything that gets in the way .... Let us keep our eyes fixed on Jesus.'

Eternal

ETERNITY is
—keeping a smile on your face till the camera clicks;
—waiting for the breakdown truck to arrive;
—waiting for the sound of a key in the lock at 2 a m;
—listening to a six year old relate the plot of an exciting film.

Behind these light-hearted definitions is the idea that eternity has to do with a period of time that is, or at least seems, very long. But *eternal* life as John in his Gospel conceives it, has more to do with quality and transformation of life, rather than mere extension of it.

Others think of *eternal* life as what starts when life on this earth ends, whereas again it would be more in accord with biblical teaching if we were to think of *eternal* life as what happens when real life begins. The Bible speaks of the glories of the life to come, where pain, tears and suffering are no more, but it speaks even more about enriched quality of life here and now. Jesus came, not primarily to get us into heaven, but to get more of heaven into us and our society. *Eternal* life is a different quality of life that we can experience *now*. 'I am come,' said Jesus, 'that you might have life and have it in all its fullness.' Jesus believed not only in life after death, but in life *before* death.

The Greek word *aionios*, sometimes translated *eternal*, sometimes 'everlasting', literally means 'that which befits God,' that which is akin to the divine. There is really only one person who can be described by the adjective *eternal*: that is God. Eternal life is life which has a kinship with the divine. Likewise eternal punishment is punishment which befits God, which befits a loving Father. There might have been fewer hell-fire and thunder preachers had more people realised this.

John says, 'We have crossed over from death to life. This we know because we love our brothers' (1 John 3:14, NEB). John is speaking about life here and now. Whereas self-centredness is a principle of death, caring love is the distinctive quality of eternal life. Eternal life involves broadening the horizon of our concerns to include the needs of others. It involves giving up our centrality in order to find our true centre in God and in a community of love. It involves being alive to God, to people, to human need, to beauty and truth. It involves looking at the world through the eyes of Jesus Christ.

We misunderstand eternal life if we think of it primarily in terms of life of infinite duration. Life that simply went on forever could as easily be hell as heaven. Heaven as sometimes represented could easily turn out to be something of a bore. A short story entitled *Well I'm Damned* speaks of a rich angling enthusiast who, after death, finds himself beside a small trout pool, with a helpful ghillie by his side. He casts and immediately catches a fine two-pounder. 'Well, I'm damned,' he says with satisfaction, and casts again. Another two-pounder; and a third, and a thirty-third, and a three hundred and thirty-third. By now he is saying, 'I'm damned' in quite a different tone. This is to be his hell—condemned to his own limited idea of pleasure.

Continued existence without transformation, without the ennobling of our desires, without a worthwhile purpose, without loving and being loved, could quickly pall. I prefer to speak of eternal life as timeless rather than endless. When people speak of the timeless beauty of the Highlands, they mean it is a beauty of which you do not weary. What the Gospel is saying in effect is that life need not become stale. With God's help the quality of life can be such that not even an eternity of it would be boring.

Eternal life has greater *breadth*—wide outlooks, far-ranging interests, inclusive sympathies, ourselves no longer the focal point around which all is organised.

It has greater *depth*—deep foundations, resources which go below the surface of life and tap refreshing springs. 'Those who look to the Lord will win new strength ... they will march on and never grow faint' (Isaiah 40:31, NEB). It also has deeper motivation. As well as hearing the cry of the needy, we also hear Christ saying, 'In as much as you have done it unto one of the least of these, you have done it unto me' (Matthew 25:40).

It has greater *height*. The Bible associates the idea of God with life's peak moments—with peace and serenity, vigour and victory, deliverance and inner joy.

It has greater *length*. Eternal life which begins now, will one day, said Jesus, widen into a fullness of joy and glory that we cannot as yet even begin to comprehend. 'Eye hath not seen, nor ear heard, nor has it entered into the heart of man to conceive what God has prepared for them that love him' (1 Corinthians 2:9). Of one thing we can be certain: those whose lives reflect those qualities which characterised the life of Jesus—caring love, thankfulness, the forgiving spirit, humility—will quickly feel at home in heaven.

Father

IS the universe friendly? Is there a presence behind the mystery of life? Is there another like ourselves, and yet unlike us; or is there nothing but blind chance? If there is a Creator of all things, how are we to think of him? Does he care about what happens to us or is he indifferent? People in every generation have asked these questions, their answers making up the faiths, philosophies and creeds of humankind.

Jesus believed and taught that behind life there is one whom we can call 'our heavenly *Father.*' (Heaven being synonymous with perfection, then the phrase 'heavenly *Father*' essentially means 'perfect *Father*'). And how that thought changed the mental climate of the world—the conviction that behind life, behind the world, there is one who is kindly disposed towards us. 'When you pray,' said Jesus, 'say *Our Father.*' Jesus took the word *father* and taught us to use it to describe the Creator of all things.

Jesus was more a picture book theologian than a systematic one. He likened God to a farmer going forth to sow, to a shepherd looking for lost sheep. But his key word picture was 'heavenly Father.' Now admittedly the word *father* is a very human word to describe One who completely transcends all earth-bound concepts and categories. But it is the least inadequate word we possess to describe the unseen Author of time and space. God has more in common with a perfect father than any other reality we can imagine. In using the word *father* Jesus was highlighting the fact that God is One with whom we can have personal dealings, One who is approachable and understanding.

Jesus was not thinking of God in any man-sized sense,

or as being masculine as distinct from feminine. In the
Bible there are many feminine metaphors for the grace
and love of God. We read in Isaiah: 'As one whom his
mother comforts, so will I comfort you' (66:13). Moses also
draws the analogy of God as Mother. He once watched
a mother eagle hovering around her nest trying to tempt
her fledgling to fly. But the little fellow, not knowing yet
what eagles' wings are for, refused to leave the comfortable
nest on the craggy ledge. With a sudden swoop the mother
eagle struck the nest and sent the young bird hurtling into
space. The fledgling was forced to fly. When the little bird's
strength gave out, the mother swept swiftly beneath, and
took her offspring on her outstretched wings until he re-
gained his strength. Moses used that picture as an analogy
of God. 'As an eagle stirreth up her nest, fluttereth over
her young ... so the Lord ... ' (Deuteronomy 32:11)—ie,
the motherly care of God.

We once had as neighbours an elderly Jewish couple.
When their son married a Gentile, his father effectively
disowned him. He was not allowed to return home. How
his mother agonised. She yearned for reconciliation. She
would gladly have welcomed him back, but her husband
would not allow it. The God whom Jesus revealed had more
in common with that mother than that father.

The picture Jesus paints of God in his parable of the
father and the two sons, stands in marked contrast to that
of a first century Middle Eastern father. By asking for his
inheritance while his father was still alive, the younger
son was in effect saying to his father, 'Why don't you drop
dead,' for an inheritance was only obtainable in a Jewish
family on the death of parents. Such an insult would nor-
mally have resulted in the lad being expelled from home.
Those who first heard this story must have been staggered
to hear that the father actually grants the son's request. In
the days that followed, while the son discovered what many

before and after have discovered, that the far country seldom fulfils its promise, his father endures probably the deepest pain known to the human spirit: the agony of rejected love. Each day the father gazed down the road to see if there was any sign of the lad returning. Finally one day he glimpsed in the distance a sad decrepit figure approaching. Recognising his son from the way he walked, he uttered a loud heart-cry and ran through the village street to meet and greet him. He *ran,* even though this would expose him to the mockery of the villagers: in Jesus' day 'gentlemen' never ran, they always moved at a stately pace.

The parable goes on to tell how next the older son deeply insults his father by refusing to enter the banquet hall where his father's guests were gathered. Though publicly humiliated by his older son's refusal, the father still addresses him as *teknon,* meaning my 'beloved son.'

There are parallels to Christian teaching within the world's religious literature, but there is no picture of God to compare with this portrait. Jesus communicated his distinctive message about God as *father* not only by his words, but also by his life. 'He who has seen me has seen the Father' (John 14:9). Throughout his ministry he revealed the compassion, heartbreak, loneliness and anger of God. The night before Jesus died, he told Philip that those who had seen him, now knew what kind of a father God is.

I recall one winter night visiting a rural community near Dornoch. It was so dark that nothing was visible. Suddenly out of the clouds came a lightning flash. During the split second it lasted, the whole landscape was lit up. The hills, the Dornoch Firth and the scattered crofts, all became visible. Then the darkness closed in again. I sometimes think of Christ as that lightning flash, revealing for a short time the fatherly heart and motherly concern that lie at the heart of the apparent darkness and mystery of our world. As Jesus the Son was in time, God the Father is in eternity.

Glory

SECOND Isaiah, a man of extraordinary faith, was concerned to lift his fellow exiles in Babylonia (present day Iraq) out of the slough of despond. He sought to do this by sharing with them some thoughts about the *glory* of God, by painting a memorable picture of a very great God holding our Lilliputian world in the palm of his hand, a God who 'set limits to the heavens with a span, who weighs the hills in his jeweller's scales,' a God to whom 'coasts and islands weigh as light as specks of dust' (Isaiah 40:12*f*).

As a result of the Gulf War most people now know what Babylon looks life—much of it flat, unattractive, desert land. There were no hills to which the Jewish exiles could lift up their eyes and be reminded of the faithfulness of God. Yet as the prophet reminds them, there is still the glorious night sky. 'Lift up your eyes on high and behold who created these things.'

The glory of God revealed in the heavens is a common biblical theme. The Psalmist says, 'the heavens tell out the glory of God, the vault of heaven reveals his handiwork' (Psalm 19:1, NEB). And this in an age when the universe, as the Hebrews conceived it, was a mere pinpoint compared to the awesome universe we know it to be today.

Isaiah then goes on to comfort his broken-hearted, discouraged contemporaries by telling them that their troubles are almost over, that deliverance from an apparently hopeless situation was at hand. God will use the Persian king Cyrus to break the stranglehold of Babylon and make it possible for a humbler and wiser Jewish nation to return home. Thus, he said, 'the glory of the Lord will be revealed.'

In our day, such has been the influence of Handel's Oratorio *The Messiah*, that these familiar words, 'And the glory of the Lord shall be revealed,' immediately conjure up thoughts, not of the return of the Jewish exiles from Babylon to Jerusalem, but of the coming of Jesus of Nazareth.

Over a hundred years ago, Julia Howe wrote a hymn which stirred the American people. The hymn brings together different understandings of the glory of God. The first verse speaks of glory in terms of awesome power and might:

> *Mine eyes have seen the glory of the coming of the Lord,*
> *He is trampling out the vintage where the grapes of*
> *   wrath are stored,*
> *He hath loosed the fatal lightning of his terrible swift*
> *   sword,*
> *Our God is marching on.*

But in the third verse we are reminded that there is another aspect to divine glory, the kind of glory revealed in the life of Jesus:

> *In the beauty of the lilies Christ was born across the sea,*
> *With a glory in his bosom that transfigures you and me.*

In the introduction to his Gospel, John tells how the One who inhabits eternity came to dwell in time, how the Creator of all things put himself at the mercy of the people he created. 'The Word became flesh' and we beheld his glory 'not full of might and terror,' but 'full of grace and truth.' For Christians God is no longer just the immense power that created the heavens—no longer just the mighty force that fashioned Ben Nevis and Mount Everest—no longer just the energy that ultimately directs

the march of history. God now has a human face—the
face of Jesus of Nazareth. What a glorious life his was,
the kind of life we would like every life to be—fruitful
and well spent, a life characterised by courage, grace
and winsome goodness. There was certainly nothing drab
or petty or killjoy about it.

It has been suggested that glory is to God what style
is to the artist. To behold God's glory is to sense his style.
In the Bethlehem manger, the workshop at Nazareth,
on Mount Calvary and the road to Emmaus, God's glory
—his unique style—became visible to the naked eye. The
style contrasted sharply with the Messianic style envi-
sioned by the Jews. The divine action that first Christmas
took place not in a palace, not even in an inn, but in an
unpretentious outhouse. The Jews thought of glory in terms
of 'crowns', 'robes', 'banners', 'trumpets' and 'processions.'
But Jesus did not come with a sword in his hand, nor with
pomp and ceremony, but with incredible compassion in
his heart for the distressed and the downtrodden. His life
was devoted to redeeming what people had ruined, to
tearing down the racial, religious and class barriers they
had erected.

Jesus' life was proof that *glory* is to be thought of more
in terms of lowly service than in terms of great power or
wealth or status. 'Among you whoever wants to be great,
must be your servant' (Mark 10:44, NEB). In Jesus, holding
out hands of help and healing, befriending those who had
no friends, uttering that ineffably tender prayer, 'Father
forgive them' (not 'Father strike them down'), we glimpse
true glory.

Grace

GRACE is one of the most distinctive words in the Christian vocabulary. It rings like music through the New Testament and through many hymns. Although centuries of handling and mishandling have resulted in religious words like *sin, salvation* and *conversion* becoming shop-worn, *grace* has fared better than most. Even its derivatives, *graciousness* and *graceful* still retain something of their original splendour.

Though the words *grace* and *gratitude* come from the same Latin root, and though today 'saying *grace*' essentially means 'saying thanks', yet *grace* in the New Testament means much more than gratitude. It also means more than charm and winsomeness. *Grace* is love that is not deserved, love for the unlovely, love at its most generous. When we say 'God is gracious', we mean God loves us, not just when we accomplish something worthwhile, but even when we mess things up. The cowboy benediction, 'May the good Lord take a likin' to you', is bad theology. God goes on loving us even when we break his commandments and his heart.

The Gospel writers tell us that Jesus Christ, who was 'full of grace,' never spoke 'except in parables.' Following his example, let me share with you two stories which illustrate powerfully what grace means.

A father tells how once in the middle of the night he found his broken-hearted wife kneeling beside their son's bed. The lad lay there fully clothed, having once again returned in a drunken stupor. His wife was stroking her son's hair. Looking up, she said, through her tears, 'He won't let me love him when he is awake.' Though her love was not deserved, she kept on loving. This is grace.

George Romney, the brilliant young English painter, was misled by Sir Joshua Reynolds into thinking that marriage and parenthood spoiled an artist. So he abandoned his wife and two children and went to London. When old, desolate and nearly mad, he returned to Kendal and to his wife. She received him with amazing grace, nursing him with devotion until he died three years later. In his poem about Romney, 'Romney's Remorse', Lord Tennyson pictures the elderly artist, wondering who it is that nurses him with so gentle a touch. The poem is as much about the healing power of grace as about the destructive power of human selfishness.

So too is Jesus' parable about the lad who broke with his father and left home. The details of the story are well known: the wrong crowd, the late hours, the free life. The far country was in the prodigal's mind long before he ever set out for it. The father pleaded with his son, but finally had to let him go. He aged rapidly. There was a great sadness in his eyes. His friends told him that for his health's sake, he must not take it so hard. 'Oh I know,' he said, 'I know other youngsters go wrong, but to think that John, my John should!'

It is all so modern. Many parents of teenagers are trying desperately to hold on to certain standards which they feel are basic, while trying at the same time to give their young people freedom to make their own decisions. The parents sometimes end up feeling that their love has been despised and defeated.

There are two prodigals in the story which Jesus told—the lad who in the far country lost his bearings, honour, money and self-respect; but also the father who, according to the elder brother, was wasting his love. The father is the real prodigal, running to meet his son, kissing him, calling for new shoes and a ring for his finger: 'Bring forth the best robe' (Luke 15:22). The lad's dirty, tattered clothes reflected his inner nature. The 'best robe' symbolised the restoring of dignity and sense of worth. What a commentary the parable is on the amazing grace of God.

When youngsters are reprimanded, they sometimes say 'sorry' in such a way that it is obvious they are anything but sorry. When the sorrow is genuine, however, when it is clear that the child genuinely regrets what he or she has done, and wants to make a fresh start, parents will often wrap the child in forgiveness. 'Look son,' they say, 'We will stand by you. We will live down the shame of it together.' That is grace.

A few years ago an American Rabbi, Harold Kushner, wrote a book which is well worth reading—*When bad things happen to good people.* Perhaps one day he will write a sequel—*When good things happen to bad people*—for that also often happens. We call it grace.

One of the reasons why St Paul spoke so often about 'the grace of our Lord Jesus Christ' was because he had experienced the reality of undeserved love in his own life. For years he had denied Jesus' claims, blasphemed his name and persecuted his followers. When he was confronted with the Risen Christ on the road to Damascus, he might well have expected Jesus to say, 'Just you wait. You will pay for this.' But instead, Christ said in effect, 'Look Saul, I still want you on my side.' That day the grace of the Lord Jesus Christ became compelling and real for Saul.

In *Beauty and the Beast,* when the beast discovers that Beauty really loves him, despite his ugliness, he begins to become more beautiful. Likewise, when a person discovers that God loves him despite his unloveliness, that person often becomes more of a gracious and healing influence in the world.

Holy Spirit

WHEN Christian ministers or priests celebrate the Sacrament of the Lord's Supper, they say a prayer before repeating the actual practice of Jesus in breaking bread and raising a cup. In that prayer they ask God to 'send his *Holy Spirit*' to 'sanctify' the elements of bread and wine on the table, so that they may become to the believer, the Body and Bread of Christ. What, or who, is this *Holy Spirit*?

From the 4th century AD the Church has felt itself impelled to speak of the *Holy Spirit* as inseparable from God, as God in action. This has arisen from the need to describe the presence of God with us now, in contemporary experience, rather than simply to speak of God objectively—'as he is in himself'—in his utter mystery and otherness. The working out of a doctrine of the *Holy Spirit* across the centuries of Christian thought and reflection has been a far more complex task than might be supposed, given that all Christians agree on the immediacy of the experience of *Holy Spirit* in their lives. You would think that in this one area all would be simplicity itself. Indeed when the confused academic Nicodemus slipped along the alleyways under cover of darkness to speak to Jesus of his religious uncertainties (John 3), Jesus immediately redirected him to think of the Spirit in the most vivid visual terms: 'Listen to the wind, Nicodemus. So is everyone who is born of the Spirit.'

Jesus himself, in speaking of God's Spirit, is using a picture, an analogy: the wind, and the mystery of its movement. It is indeed very difficult to speak of the Holy Spirit except in picture-words, or images. Augustine worked through to his famous 'Social Analogy': God as the Lover, Christ as the Beloved, and the Holy Spirit as the Love between them. Others have used words like 'breathing', 'pouring', 'pervading', 'filling', in an attempt to catch the quintessentiality of the Spirit of God in action. However, all human images have limitations, and those who wish to drive coaches and horses through them can do so.

The Church found itself compelled, from early days, to speak of God in terms of 'Three Persons in Unity.' The Holy Spirit is the 'third' Person of the Trinity, but only 'third' in the sense in which, with our poor human vocabulary, we have to find a way of speaking of how God impinges upon us. There are difficulties with the word 'Person.' One can grasp how God has to be spoken of in 'personal' terms, and certainly Jesus is a Person. But the mind gets confused trying to grasp how the 'bond' between them can be spoken of as 'a Person.' The Church Fathers, and their successors, were determined not to speak of God's Spirit in impersonal terms: *ie,* as an 'it', rather than a 'he.' They wished to preserve the special activity of God from confusion with 'spirits' (with which the world was thought to abound), or with abstractions and 'ideas' in some Greek philosophical sense. It was this crude material misunderstanding which Jesus countered when he spoke to the Samaritan woman at Jacob's well (John 4): 'God is a Spirit, and those who worship *him* must worship *him* in Spirit and in Truth.'

The Church teaches that the Holy Spirit is the special gift given at Pentecost, after Christ's physical removal from the apostles and friends. Gathered together in one place, they suddenly 'experienced' God in a new, powerful interior way which did not require 'external' verification. They also 'understood' each other in a new way, a way indescribably wonderful. Those who, like Luke, attempted to describe it, were compelled, again, to use the language of imagery —rushing wind, tongues of fire, ecstasy, and so on. They all *knew* it was the presence of Christ with them, in a

new way, yet in a way that was consistent with the Christ
with whom they had walked and talked in Galilee.

Those who tried to cheat the new vision—to take advantage of it—like Ananias and Sapphira, were spoken of
as 'lying to the Holy Spirit.' Saul of Tarsus is unhorsed and
blinded so that he might be 'filled with the Holy Spirit.'
The great early Christian Letters—Romans; 1, 2 Corinthians—are permeated from beginning to end with references
to the Spirit, vivid evidence of God as 'experienced.' The
Holy Spirit is the living presence of Christ working in the
believer. As such, the 'work' of the Spirit is to give life
and effect change from evil to goodness. And so the Holy
Spirit brings about the great alterations—from enmity to
reconciliation; from living in deceit to living in a state of
grace; from bondage to freedom. 'Where the Spirit of the
Lord is, there is liberty' (2 Corinthians 3:17). The 'fruits'
of the Spirit in a person or community are 'love, joy,
peace, patience, kindness, goodness, faithfulness, humility and self-control' (Galatians 5:22), as opposed to the
cankered fruit born from unspiritual human nature.

There have always been groups in the Church who
manipulate the Holy Spirit and consider it their own pre-
rogative. Even in the earliest days, the Churches fell prey
to a false 'enthusiasm' and claimed that the Holy Spirit
was especially at work among them. This is still a great
danger in parts of the worldwide Church and is very difficult to control. On the other hand there are Churches from
whom the Holy Spirit (the Spirit of life, energy, change,
passion, warmth, liberty, risk) seems to have departed,
Churches cramped in wintry formalisms and petrified
structures. The test of the presence of the Holy Spirit is
whether the life and love of Jesus Christ, as known in the
Gospels, is truthfully reflected. To use an old and biblical
phrase, the Spirit 'takes the things of Christ and makes
them ours.' That wonderful phrase invites long reflection.

Hope

CHRISTIANS and non-Christians both use the word *hope* frequently. They use it in casual conversation in the same way: '*Hope* to see you at the match next Saturday!' It's one of these indispensable little words we almost feel we don't need to define. We know in our bones what *hope* is, don't we? An attitude of confident and good expectation about the future—something like that. Some would say that *hope* is an indispensable attribute of the human condition: '*Hope* springs eternal in the human breast'; 'Where there is life, there's *hope*.' Not to *hope* is to be *hopeless*, and to be *hopeless* is to be bereft of everything that makes life worth living.

Our conventional and idiomatic use of the word is very frequently identical to the word 'optimism': confident of better tomorrows. We hope for many things, many outcomes—a good harvest, a warm summer, a fine day for the wedding, a healthy baby, a good night's sleep after the day's activities. The human race, and each member of the human family, shares a myriad common *hopes*, and indeed it is this awareness that these hopes—both trivial and colossal, both personal and collective—are nurtured in every village and city and homestead on our planet, that gives substance and reality to the dreams of common brotherhood.

But you cannot take the Bible into your hands for very long without realising that hope is being expressed in its pages in a very different sense, and carries a much more profound cargo.

Although the biblical writers often still use the word in the conventional way (an expectation of good outcomes), *hope* is used most consistently with God as its source, its ground, its assurance, and its object. The Old Testament writers find their constant hope only in God. God alone is the, hope not only of the individual (see Psalm 62:5 —'truly my heart waits silently for God; my hope comes from him'), but also of the covenant community, and of the whole Creation. Hope resides in who God is, and what he has done.

There is no contradiction when the New Testament writers begin to speak of Christ as our hope. Many of the metaphors and images attributed to God under the Old Testament are transferred over to Christ in the New. He is a refuge and a fortress, the rock on which true hope is built. Because Christ represents God's reconciliation of the world to himself, the Christian can hope in Christ, because the Son and the Father are one.

This one hope is anchored in the divine activity, and thus covers the whole span of historical time. God is Alpha and Omega, he who creates from nothing, and he to whom the nations look for the ultimate consummation of everything. Christian hope is not simply a confident look to the future: it springs from a conviction that God is consistent with himself, and what he has been is what he will be. Biblical writers can thus speak of 'living hope' in the past tense as well as the future. 'In this hope we were saved' (Romans 8:24). Hope, that is *Christian hope*, has memory in it as well as expectation. It is a gift from God—we live in hope, because hope lives in us, since Christ 'lives in us.' Hope is not, for Christians, simply a dream about tomorrow. It is a reality that reveals the future in the past and the past in the future.

The question about the Source of Hope is an insistent and crucial one for our planet today. Just as when an individual, brought to the ground by some crisis, asks frantically if he has any grounds for hope, so the collective human consciousness seeks for reassurance in the tidal rip of our times, borne down by the sufferings which beset the planet.

There are many who claim to have gained the necessary perspective upon the total picture. The claim amounts to this: that the human race has the necessary resources *within itself* to conquer its own problems. Proponents of this resonant call to arms usually deploy their confidence on three fronts. First, there must be a global strategy, introducing economic and political co-ordination, emerging in some form of world government. Second, there must be acceleration of universal education. And third, there must be a recovery of the collective moral conscience. The *basso profundo* coming through all this is clear: mankind can cope without external aid if it organises itself speedily and efficiently.

Like all heresies, the quotient of truth contained is high. On all these fronts, urgent development and reconstruction is vital. But Christians know that the source and ground of hope lies nowhere in ourselves, nor in resources we can harness. Our hope, our true ground of hope, is in God. The message of the Incarnation will never get a hearing so long as we continue to delude ourselves that we can solve our problems by our own energy and cleverness. God has visited and redeemed his people. That is the source of our hope, and that alone. Of course political, economic, educational and moral imperatives follow immediately and most urgently. But the fundamental need of all of us is to hear, and hear again, and be changed in the inner heart *of us*. The divine strategy—so different from our human strategies—is to come to us in such a way that we can know what Love is, and what Love costs, and what Love asks. And when we pick that up, we hold in our hands the seeds of hope for our world.

Immortality

I THINK of a mother known to me whose son of twenty was killed in an accident on the other side of the world; no one seems able to share her sense of desolation, and she desperately wants to know that her dearly loved son is all right. She has been tempted to look to spiritualism in an attempt to find the reassurance she needs that her son is well, and we can all understand the earnestness of her desire. Along that road, however, there often lies disappointment and disillusionment, fulfilling the words of Kipling:

> *Oh the road to En-dor is the oldest road*
> *and the craziest road of all!*
> *Straight it leads to the witch's abode,*
> *As it did in the days of Saul,*
> *And nothing has changed of the sorrow in store*
> *For such as go down on the road to En-dor!*

I am sure that the bewilderment and grief we know at such times can be eased if we take time to think of what the Bible has to say about immortality.

The word *immortality* and the related word *immortal* only occur three times in the Good News Bible version of the New Testament, because the New Testament prefers to speak of 'eternal life' or simply of 'life.' We think of *immortality* or eternal life as the reality which lies beyond the gate which we call death, but in the New Testament, and in John's Gospel in particular, it has quite another dimension to it.

John's Gospel speaks of eternal life *before* death. We

find this in various verses which are used to describe it. For example, when Jesus says, 'Whoever lives and believes in me will never die' (John 11:26, GNB); or when the first letter of John tells us, 'God has given us eternal life and this life has its source in his Son. Whoever has the Son has this life' (John 5:11-12, GNB). Clearly, Jesus did not mean that those who believe in him will not die, for all of us are destined to reach the end of our earthly life; what he meant was that the life he gives is not affected by that death, for it is the life of God's perfect world.

Many years ago a senior minister asked me what theology I was reading, and I told him I had just read the Narnia books by C S Lewis. I remember my senior colleague's scorn to this day! Yet in retrospect, I think he was less than fair to C S Lewis (and incidentally to me!). If you read for example *The Lion, the Witch and the Wardrobe*, you find yourself drawn into the distinctive world of C S Lewis; the children live in two worlds—the everyday, 'normal' world, and the other, exciting world of 'Narnia'. It is easy to see Narnia in terms of the 'Kingdom of God', which is the way Matthew, Mark and Luke speak of what John calls 'eternal life', and for me at least it is extraordinarily helpful.

It is related to Jesus himself. In the other Gospels, eternal life is replaced by the concept of the 'Kingdom of God' and we can say from them that eternal life is simply life in the Kingdom of Jesus: that is, life where Jesus is King. This is a life we can taste just now when we submit our own wills to his and try to live in his way—for then we are tasting the life that will be beyond the change we call death. The way to this life, Jesus tells us, is 'Knowing you, the only true God, and Jesus Christ, whom you sent.' As one of our great New Testament scholars has said, knowing God means 'acknowledging him in his works and responding to his claims.' It is when we acknowledge Jesus

as Lord and begin to respond to his claims upon us, that
we become members of his kingdom and that we share
this eternal life.

It is this that Jesus assures us will never end. Indeed,
for Christians death itself is past, because our life with Jesus
Christ is life of the nature and quality of eternity. Some
years ago an elderly gentleman in our congregation died;
I went straight from the funeral to see his wife, whose own
health had prevented her from being present at the service.
I had no sooner returned home than the phone rang; it was
their daughter to say that her mother had just died. That
night, one of the grandchildren asked his father what had
happened to Gran and Grandpa; looking round the bed-
room, the father saw the boy's clothes lying over a chair.
He said, 'When you went to bed tonight, you took off your
clothes and put them away, and then got into bed. Gran
and Grandpa have just put away the bodies they used, and
they have gone to heaven.' How right he was: for his parents
were not dead, but alive. And the life they had entered was
a continuation of all that was theirs in Christ during their
time on earth. Immortality is not just something awaiting
us beyond death, but something Jesus offers to us now
when he offers us 'Life in all its fullness.'

Incarnation

THE common use of the word *incarnation* refers to the life of Jesus of Nazareth from his birth at Bethlehem to his death upon the Cross. The idea behind it is that God entered human life in the person of Jesus in fulfilment of the promise of Jesus' birth: 'His name shall be called Immanuel, which means God is with us'(Matthew 1:23, GNB). For many people this is impossible to grasp.

It is important for us to realise that the *incarnation* was not something which theologians thought up; it was something which the first followers of Jesus discovered for themselves. It was when the disciples lived with Jesus, watched him, listened to him, and learned from him, that the realisation began to dawn that this was no ordinary person. It was from their experience that they worked out who he had to be, and they came to the conclusion that this person Jesus was both fully man and, at the same time, fully God.

How can one person be both God and man? This is at the heart of our difficulties with the idea of the *incarnation*. I find it helpful to acknowledge that in the person of Jesus we find ourselves drawn beyond the limits of our minds. To say that Jesus is both man and God can be likened to saying '1 + 1 =1'; it is literally *absurd*, beyond the reach of our minds—and we are tempted to try to simplify it by saying that while he was God, he was not really a man; or on the other hand, that he was indeed fully human, but not really divine.

Yet the New Testament has no doubt; Jesus meets us in its pages as a complete human being: he becomes tired, he can weep, he eats and drinks, he befriends people. But at the same time the New Testament uses quite remarkable language to say that he is divine. One word is translated 'exact likeness' (it is the word for the ruler's image on a coin, or for an artist's portrait of his subject), meaning that when we look at Jesus, we see what God is like. The late William Barclay said to me during my student days, 'If I had to sum up the New Testament in one sentence I would say: God is like Jesus.' That is profoundly true for the Christian; and Jesus himself said, 'Whoever has seen me has seen the Father' (John 14:9, GNB).

Charles Simeon, a Cambridge scholar, once said something that is profoundly true: 'The truth lies, not in one extreme or in the other, nor in the middle; it lies in both extremes.' There is no keyword of the faith where that is more applicable than the incarnation. The glory of the incarnation is not simply that Jesus came to show what man could become, or just to teach man how he ought to live; it is that in Jesus, God has entered human life to put right what had gone wrong. We find it beyond our understanding how this could be, and yet the New Testament insists upon its truth.

An old countryman was once attacked by an atheist who asked him, 'Pray, my good fellow, tell me: is your God a little God, or a large God?' 'Sir,' answered the countryman, 'he is so great that the heaven of heavens cannot contain him, and so little that he can live within my heart.'

I think he got it right!

Messiah (Christ)

THESE two words mean the same: *Messiah* is the Hebrew, *Christ* is the Greek, meaning 'the anointed one.' Peter, we are told, was the one to make the connection with Jesus when he said, 'You are the *Messiah*, the Son of the living God' (Matthew 16:16, GNB).

The word meant a great deal to the Jews of the first century, as the *Messiah* figure was their hope for the restoration of Israel; however, the word meant very little to the Roman population and to the others in the ancient world. When Christians said 'Jesus is Lord,' they made a statement which in later years came to be regarded as treasonable; but when they said 'Jesus is the *Christ* or the *Messiah*,' it was almost a coded word which meant a great deal to those of Jewish faith, but little to those outside.

In a modern setting, it is a word that says a great deal about Jesus to those who know and trust in him, but it is also a word that is meaningless—even used as a swear word—to those with little faith. We can get at the meaning of the name by thinking more of the derivation—by looking at those who were 'anointed' in the Old Testament, which forms the living background to the New Testament. There were three such persons.

The first was the *prophet*. We have many instances of prophets in the Old Testament. Their job was not to foretell the future, but to proclaim the Word of God. This frequently involved a kind of foretelling similar to us telling our children, 'If you touch the fire, you will be burned'—but the foretelling was simply a consequence of speaking God's message. Jesus filled the prophet's role, for he spoke from God.

The second person, the *priest*, was also anointed: his
task was two-fold: to be God's representative among men,
and to be man's representative before God. The letter of the
Hebrews speaks of Jesus as 'our great High Priest' (4:14,
GNB), who understands what life is like for us; in addition
it tells that he has also 'entered the presence of God,' and
that he prays for his people. We can catch something of
the content of that prayer when we read John chapter 17,
which indeed is often called 'The High Priestly Prayer.'

The third anointing, then as now, was of the *sovereign*.
Just as our Queen was anointed at her coronation, so the
Old Testament kings were anointed, sometimes publicly,
sometimes (like David) privately. The anointing sealed
the authority they were given. When Jesus began his ministry, we are told by Mark that he said, 'The Kingdom
of God is near!' (Mark 1:15, GNB), and on the Cross he
suffered under the placard which read 'Jesus of Nazareth,
King of the Jews.'

So, to refer to Jesus as the *Christ*, or the *Messiah*, is
to acknowledge him as prophet, priest and king. It is interesting to note that it was after Peter's statement, 'You
are the *Messiah*' (Matthew 16:16, GNB), when Jesus spoke
of building his Church on the rock foundation of that
faith. It is a complete faith; it acknowledges the truth of
Jesus' teaching; it rejoices in his understanding of us and
his prayer for us; and it submits to his authority. Understood in its fullness, the sentence 'Jesus is the *Christ*'
is a concise summary of what we believe about him as
Saviour and Lord.

Prayer

IT is with considerable hesitancy that I write about *prayer*, for not only is there much about *prayer* that I do not understand, but my own *prayer* life is so faulty and flawed. Yet write I must, for *prayer* is a keyword of faith. The activity we call *prayer* is at the heart of the Christian religion.

Living as we do in a culture that is not used to stillness, and in a secular society where many regard faith in God as out-dated and prayer as self-deception, it is perhaps not surprising that the things of the spirit are not very real to many people, and that only in times of extremity does private prayer have any place in their lives. The pagan nonsense often talked about prayer has further aggravated the situation. Joe Oldham tells of a man who one night prayed that he might have a comfortable journey by train the following day. When he managed to get a corner seat despite the train being crowded, he was certain God had granted his request. He wrote to the local paper telling of his answered prayer. A few days later another letter appeared, written by a man who had travelled on the same train. He told how he too had got a corner seat *without praying about it*, but that he later gave it to a lady who was standing in the corridor!

It concerns me that many today subconsciously think of prayer either as a grocery list that you telephone to Heaven's Supermarket, God being the errand-boy to deliver the goods, or as a spare tyre which is really of no interest until a blow-out lets you down.

It is a tragedy prayer should have been so misrepresented and neglected, for we all need to pray, to take thought about life's meaning, to wrestle regularly with what the

will of God means for us and our world, to replenish our
too soon exhausted store of kindness and serenity. We all
need to turn from controlling things to the one by whom
we ought to be controlled. We need to open our lives to
the Spirit of love and power that permeates the universe.
In prayer we have the means of restoring some degree of
wholeness and purpose to our lives.

The term *prayer* has several meanings. We misunderstand Paul's instruction to 'pray without ceasing' (1
Thess. 5:17) if we think it means 'saying prayers without
ceasing.' Paul, who always gave his undivided attention
to the work he had to do, was here thinking of prayer as
an attitude in which we are unconsciously conscious of
God as a child is of its mother. Paul's life was dominated
by the desire to know and do God's will; his plans were
dependent for fulfilment on divine help, but he was not
always consciously thinking of God. Paul knew that we
pray most really when we live most deeply, that prayer
is less the performance of certain rites than the uplifting
of the whole personality to God—a developing sensitivity
to the 'other' dimension in life—the power and love behind what we see and feel. Prayer is bringing our littleness
close to God's greatness, our ignorance close to God's
wisdom, our weakness close to God's strength, and our
self-centredness close to God's forgiving love.

In Kathryn Hulme's book, *The Nun's Story,* the Mother
Superior of the hospital in which Sister Luke began her
nursing career, says to the young nurses, 'All for Jesus ...
say it, my dear students, every time you are called on for
what seems an impossible task. Say it for the bed-pans
you carry, for the old incontinents you bathe, for those
sputum cups of the tubercular.' Then, as Mother Superior
bent over a patient to change a dressing foul with corruption,
she said to the sister, 'All for Jesus ... this is no beggar's
body picked up in the Rue des Radis. This is the body of

Christ and this suppurating sore is one of his wounds.' To think thus is to pray. To regard the little things we are called on to do as our service to God at that moment, is to live in the attitude of prayer.

For Jesus, prayer as an attitude and as a discipline were complementary. Matthew tells us how he told his followers to 'go into their room and pray to their Father' (6:6). Luke tells us that on the Sabbath he went to the synagogue as 'his custom was' (4:16). There he joined in the prayers and worship of the local congregation. For Jesus, prayer was a corporate as well as an individual activity.

The nature of the private prayer life of Jesus was so different from the long mechanical, stereotyped prayers of the Pharisees, that it awakened in the disciples a new desire to pray: 'Lord teach us to pray' (Luke 11:1). The model prayer which Jesus taught them contained only 67 words. He obviously did not regard long-windedness as a virtue in prayer.

If we are to live each day in the attitude of prayer, it is helpful to set aside definite moments when we focus our mind on God and what he would have us do

— On wakening to thank God for the new day;
— Starting work at our desk, bench or sink, to ask for strength and grace for what we have to do;
— Returning home, to ask God to accept and bless the good we have done and forgive any mistakes we have made;
— Before we sleep, to think for a little about God, and the needs of those about whom we ought to be concerned.

Prayer as an attitude and a discipline are complementary.

'When you pray,' said Jesus, 'say Our Father ....' (Matthew 6:9). It is significant that Jesus did not say much about the technique of prayer. He spoke far more about

God. He knew that the mental picture we have of God conditions our prayers and determines our expectations. The story of the garden of Gethsemane is a powerful reminder that God bears no resemblance to the fairy at the wishing well. There Jesus fell on his face and prayed earnestly that the suffering which lay ahead of him might somehow be averted. But his request did not prevail. And neither will our requests automatically succeed. God does not say like Aladdin's genie, 'Your wish is my command.'

We degrade prayer when we think of it as a slick way of dumping every problem in God's lap and then sitting back, or as a means of imposing our will on God's, or as holding up a filled-in cheque for God to sign. Prayer is rather the means whereby we seek to open up our minds and hearts to the promised help and guidance of God. In a book about Mother Teresa, Malcolm Muggeridge wrote, 'Pray and your heart will grow big enough to receive Him.' Instead of being a substitute for thinking and working, prayer helps us to have nobler thoughts and do better work. Prayer is not a tool by which we talk God into changing all our problems into peaches and cream. Rather it is a tool by which we allow God to talk to us about what he wants us to do. The older I become, the more I pray, 'Lord use me' or 'change me' or 'strengthen me,' instead of '*Gimme.*'

How often God has used the dimension of silence and the medium of quiet contemplation to make himself known. A brief period of devotional reading can help us make the transition from the hectic world of daily routine, and from the problems which have such a hold on our minds. Many who turn to prayer only in times of crisis, are so obsessed by what has happened that the crisis, rather than God, dominates their thoughts even as they pray. On the other hand, those who have previously learned how to meditate on God find contemplative silence a great solace in time of extremity. They know how to call their thoughts in from the problem and think instead of God's goodness, faithfulness, wisdom and power. This is the golden key to prayer: *thinking more about God than our own problems.* By focussing our minds on a biblical passage such as Psalm 23, 'The Lord is my shepherd, I shall not want'; or a biblical phrase such as 'Nothing in all creation can separate us from the love of God' (Romans 8:39); or 'When you pass through the waters I will be with you' (Isaiah 43:2); many have found healing and renewed hope. There is a close link between prayerful meditation and medication.

When the Reverend Dr Joseph Parker was once mockingly asked, 'What did God do for Stephen as he faced death by stoning at the hands of that angry Jewish mob?,' his reply was: 'He enabled Stephen to say, "Lord lay not this sin to their charge"' (Acts 7:60). Prayer did not bring about a stay of Stephen's execution, but it did enable him to die like his Lord, forgiving his enemies. And when Saint Francis of Assisi prayed that he might be a faithful instrument of God, he did not alter God's purpose, but he did release it—and through Saint Francis there was a fresh invasion of the world by God.

Redemption

TO *redeem* something is to 'buy it back'—and the most frequent use of the word today is in the context of the pawnbroker's shop. We know that it is a word connected with money and payment, and so we may well feel uncomfortable when we find it also used in the Bible. The word is used some 17 times in the New Testament, in such verses as Mark 10:45 where we are told by Jesus that he came 'to give his life to *redeem* many people.' Now we understand that the word stresses the *cost* of the Cross, but it leads to problems when we think of 'buying back,' as if God bought us back from someone.

We find difficulty with the word because we instinctively associate it with the money market, and with the old stories we loved as children where the King paid a ransom for the release of the Prince. If we are to understand the meaning of redemption today, we need to remember that our New Testament has its roots not in the world of fairy tales, but in the robust life of the Old Testament.

When we turn to the book of Exodus, we learn that God redeemed his people from Egypt; and the emphasis is on *what God did*. The best illustration of what redemption means is in the lovely story of the book of Ruth: there we learn of the young widow Ruth coming to Bethlehem with her mother-in-law Naomi. They are hard up, and Ruth goes to glean in the fields for food. While there, she is noticed by a man called Boaz, a distant relation of her late husband (you really have to read the story in full to get the flavour of it). Eventually Boaz marries Ruth. So a rags-to-riches story takes place, and Ruth, the girl from the alien land of Moab, is brought into the bloodline of the royal house of David. (According to Matthew 1:6, she was David's great grandmother).

The interesting point is that the word used to describe Boaz (usually translated 'kinsman') is the word for *redeemer*; according to this book, Boaz *redeemed* Ruth. *That* is the context in which we can make sense of the imagery of redemption: Jesus redeems us by inviting us into a relationship with him which is analogous to marriage. Now in marriage there are two elements which become one: first, there is the marriage ceremony, when husband and wife take their vows; and second, there is the relationship which begins and grows over the years. The same holds good for our understanding of redemption: like marriage, it is based on something that has happened (the Cross); and like marriage, it is the beginning of a continuing life-long relationship.

What of the 'price'?—Jesus spoke of this: 'this is my blood, poured out for many for the forgiveness of sins' (Matthew 26:28, GNB). Again, the Old Testament comes to our aid, for we read in Deuteronomy 12:23 that 'the life is in the blood.' The Bible uses the imagery of blood to represent life—and the picture of the shedding of Jesus' blood means that he gave his life on the Cross; but it also refers to his present, risen life.

The trouble is that although there are these two aspects to redemption (something done in the past, and a present relationship), we tend to emphasise one or the other. The full biblical meaning of redemption is both—that Jesus died, and that Jesus lives! As someone once said, 'It is not union with the death of Christ, or with the resurrection of Christ, that matters—it is union with Christ who died and rose again, who is alive for ever.'

Repent

REPENT and *repentance* are keywords in the Christian vocabulary. They are also misunderstood words. Many equate *repentance* with feeling sorry for some foolish word or act which has caused us to lose our sleep, our licence, our job, our self-respect, or the trust of others. Why did I do it? What a fool I have been. There is however much more to the biblical understanding of *repentance* than personal regret. Paul describes the kind of remorse which concentrates primarily on the effect of our wrong-doing on ourselves as *worldly grief*. Its only value is that it indicates at least some awareness of how often we are our own worst enemy.

Genuine repentance on the other hand—or *godly grief*, as Paul calls it—involves the awareness not only of the harmful effect of our self-centredness, stupidity and greed on ourselves, but also on others. If as a result of careless driving I killed a child on the roads, the mental anguish would be awful. Greater however than the pain of the court case, or the penalty imposed, would be the realisation of the heartbreak caused to the parents and grandparents.

The Bible reminds us there is another dimension to godly grief and genuine repentance—the realisation that our behaviour hurts God. Because King David coveted Uriah's lovely wife Bathsheba, he deliberately arranged for Uriah to be posted to the front line troops in the hope that he would be killed. When David was later brought to see the enormity of what he had done, he wrote, 'Against thee have I sinned O God' (Psalm 51:4). He now realised he had not only broken God's law, but God's heart.

For the prodigal son in Jesus' story, the turning point occurs when in the piggery he stops thinking about how

much he himself was now suffering for his reckless behaviour, and begins to think about how his behaviour had
hurt his father. Only then was he on the way to genuine
repentance and recovery.

The distinction Paul makes between worldly grief and
godly grief is a valid one. Those who let their passions get
out of control, who betray their ideals and disobey their
consciences, are often, at least for a short time, thoroughly
disgusted with themselves. Sometimes they mistakenly
imagine that this indicates penitence; whereas their dis-
gust could in reality be little more than regret at being
found out. They might well do the same thing again if they
could be sure that this time they could escape the consequences.

Repentance, as the Bible conceives it, has more to do
with our attitude to the future than to the past, more to do
with a change of heart than a wallowing in self-pity.
A keyword in the Old Testament is the Hebrew term
shubh which means *turn*: 'turn to me'—'turn away from
the true to the false'—turn from being 'self-centred' to
'God-centred.' True repentance involves a radical reorient-
ation in our lifestyle. It demonstrates its regret by changed
attitudes and deeds, by seeking to mend the wretched
situation that thoughtless conduct has produced.

The word *repent* is so misunderstood that the trans-
lators of the Good News Bible felt it necessary to use instead
the phrase 'turn away from your sins.' John Newman
memorably described this change of direction. Having
spoken of how selfish pride had ruled his will, he then
wrote, 'I loved to choose and see my path. But now lead
thou me on.' Such turning affects all we think, say and
do. Sorrow for past shortcomings is combined with a de-
termination to amend our ways, and allow God to make
us instruments of his purposes in the world.

Jesus quickened the spirit of repentance by revealing

the nature of the God we hurt by our thoughtless and selfish behaviour—a forgiving Father who goes on caring for us despite the heartbreak we cause him. Paul speaks of 'the goodness of God which leads to repentance.' Calvary clearly revealed the awful pain human wrong inflicts on God.

Jesus also quickened the spirit of repentance by revealing that we were fashioned for life on a larger scale. 'The trouble with Omar Khayyam,' said G K Chesterton, 'is that he spent his whole life in the cellar and thought it was the only room in the house.' Repentance for many involves waking up to the fact that there are many other rooms in God's house; that life could be a much bigger thing than it is. The novelist Lloyd C Douglas makes Jesus say to Zaccheus, 'What did you see that made you desire to change?' 'Good Master,' he replied, 'I saw mirrored in your eyes the face of the Zaccheus I was meant to be.'

As a boy, Roland Hayes, the distinguished black singer, walked barefoot all the way from the backwoods of Georgia to Tennessee. He carried his shoes to save them. He had had no formal education, but he had a lovely voice and enjoyed singing. In a church choir in Tennessee a doctor heard him sing. The doctor was so impressed that he took the lad home and let him hear on a gramophone the voices of Caruso and Melba. Roland later wrote of that experience: 'From that night I knew I was destined to do something beyond my comprehension. It was as if something was calling me from beyond the horizon .... It was like the opening of a door through which I glimpsed the rough outline of a great purpose. A great happiness came over me. It was as if a bell rang in my soul.' Repentance has much more to do with such an enlarging and ennobling experience than with digging up bones from the past.

Repentance is closely linked to an understanding of life as God meant it to be. It has to do with turning from a superficial, self-centred life to a trusting, caring God-centred lifestyle. Repentance is an ongoing process. I believe it will keep us company to the grave. In old age we will still be making discoveries which render us ashamed of our behaviour and prejudices.

At the beginning of his Gospel, Mark tells us how 'Jesus began to preach saying, *Repent and believe the Gospel*'—not repent and be sorrowful, but repent and rejoice. For the Gospel that we are to believe is good news, not only about a forgiving God, but about what the unlikeliest people may yet become with God's help.

Resurrection

CHRISTIANS believe in life after death—or rather, in life which is unaffected by death (see *Immortality*); but the form which that life will take has always puzzled believers, who ask in much the same words as the first Christians: 'What kind of body will we have?' For some, the phrase 'the *resurrection* of the body' means that we shall live beyond death in a reconstituted body like the one we have at present. And for others the idea is quite unthinkable. How can we understand *resurrection*?

We are not our bodies: in 1954, after a road accident, I lost part of my right leg (which was, I believe, cremated in the incinerator of Glasgow's Royal Infirmary). But I am still the person I was before the accident, and I know that if other limbs were removed, I would still be 'me'. The real 'me' is not the body, but lives in the body.

The two become intertwined because other people know 'me' only through my body—appearance, walk, look, voice *etc*, are all linked with the body I have. This is true for everyone; think of someone you knew who has died, and you are *bound* to think of them in connection with the body you knew and loved—even though you know that the real person was only 'in' that body. We could say that the body is the 'vehicle of the personality,' through which the personality is expressed and recognised.

I find that helpful; and I can go on to think of the *resurrection* life as one in which our 'personality' continues —purified (for, we are told, 'we shall be like Jesus, for we shall see him as he is'), but still essentially 'you' and 'me'. The way that personality is to be recognised is not clear—but recognised it will be, and in a form suited to the world in which the *resurrection* life is lived.

We find biblical support for this in the Old Testament: when David's week-old son died, he cried 'I shall go to him, but he shall not return to me' (2 Samuel 12:23, GNB). And in the book of Job we have a most interesting passage. Job cried, 'Even after my skin is eaten by disease, although not in this body I will see God' (Job 19:26, GNB); and he adds, quite beautifully, 'I will see him with my own eyes, and he will not be a stranger.'

Clearly we have to reckon with the impossible task of describing eternal realities in words which are tied to time; Jesus found the same problem when challenged by the Sadducees (Matthew 22:23-33, GNB). We could sum up his answer by saying 'that the nature of the resurrection life is beyond our imagining', but part of the meaning must be that relationships in eternity are also purified. While in this life, marriage is an exclusive relationship where husband and wife share a closeness which they cannot share with others, in the life of eternity our relationships will be more inclusive. Whatever form our resurrected body takes, you will still be 'you,' and I will still be 'me.' It seems to me that this makes sense of the great *resurrection* chapter in 1 Corinthians 15.

Saved

FOR some people the word *saved* smacks of old-time revival meetings where, with considerable emotion and fervour, people testify as to how they were *saved* from disreputable sins. For others the word rekindles memories either of an encounter with some brash stranger who asked if we were *saved*, or of an acrimonious debate between religious groups claiming different and exclusive ways to salvation. Yet others associate the word with getting ready to die and being *saved* from some future punishment.

It was such memories and associations that prompted Robert Graves to write:

> *I do not like the Sabbath*
> *The soap-suds and the starch*
> *The troops of solemn people*
> *Who to salvation march.*

I am sorry that the word *saved* has been so devalued, for it is one of the most important and precious of all biblical words. I am sorry also it has come to sound so 'churchy,' for it is not really a 'churchy' word. In the Bible, salvation is not confined to that department of life which we call the spiritual. There it has to do with health and reconciliation, wholeness and vigour, with setting right whatever is wrong. The Hebrew verb *to save* has the root meaning *to be spacious*.

That fits in with salvation as Jesus and Paul conceived it. Salvation for them was an enlarging experience. It had to do with enriching and fulfiling life: 'O Lord, you have redeemed me,' said the Psalmist. 'You have set my feet in a large room' (Psalm 31:5, 8). Jesus said, 'I am come that you may have life and have it in all its fullness' (John 10:10, NEB).

The idea that by loving and serving God we will one day qualify for heaven, is at best a half truth. It is more in accord with Bible teaching to say that 'to love and serve God *is heaven*, on both sides of the grave.'

'How can I be what I ain't?': that common cry sheds light on the real meaning of salvation. It has to do with becoming what we are not, with life-enrichment, with being freed from that overgrown love of self which so spoils life, both for us and others. Salvation has as much to do with being freed from false pride, discourtesy, moodiness and spite—the sins of the 'elder brother'—as from the sins of 'the prodigal.'

Edgar Allan Poe has a haunting story about a room that gets smaller and smaller. At the centre of the room there is a pit waiting for the unfortunate prisoner to be inched over the edge, without a fingerhold left. For many people life is like that. It keeps closing in. It is a cramping rather than an enlarging experience. Doors are slammed in their faces. Family and financial pressures threaten to crush them. Habits formed early on, they now have difficulty breaking. They long for someone to push back the walls and restore the freedom and large horizons they have lost.

Though Paul was often confined in Roman prisons, his mind was never imprisoned there. As he gazed out through his prison bars, he thought of the wonderful things God was doing, had done and would do. He sang songs at midnight. Convinced that there was nothing in life or death that could ever separate him from the love of God, he remained calm even during an earthquake. 'Though my outward nature is decaying,' he said, 'my inward nature is renewed day by day' (2 Corinthians 4:16). Little wonder one of the jailers longed to know the secret of such a healthy outlook on life.

Salvation, the movement from lostness to fulfilment, from despair to hope, is central to the New Testament. The Gospels and Acts tell the story of enlarged and enriched lives. In the presence of Jesus many felt, for the first time, known, loved, accepted and forgiven: their lives judged, but not condemned.

I think of Simon Peter, the woman at the well in Samaria, the woman of the streets, and many others including Zaccheus. For all his outward trappings of financial success, Zaccheus was not happy. He has many twentieth century counterparts. Newspapers are full of the domestic problems of the rich and famous. Though we regularly see their fictionalised conflicts and neuroses in TV soaps, we do not seem to get the message. We remain convinced that if only we had what they have, if only we could afford to do the 'fun' things they do, and wear the clothes they wear, then we would be happy.

In the presence of Jesus, Zaccheus suddenly realised how hollow his life was, poor in the things that really matter. His former selfish ways would no longer do. That day he experienced the liberating power of a new love and loyalty: 'The half of my estate I give to the poor.' Zaccheus' contemporaries probably called such a change in outlook 'stupidity', 'recklessness' or 'financial suicide.' Jesus called it *salvation*.

Jesus still enlarges life by giving us a healthier outlook on life, a worthwhile purpose for living, and resources of spiritual vitality. These help us cope with life's setbacks. They also enable us to retain in our later years our enthusiasm for life and service. Life is enlarged when disinfected of egotism, guilt, anxiety and meaninglessness.

Salvation is not a one-off happening. It involves a lifetime of fresh starts and broadening horizons. Paul speaks of those who are 'being saved' (1 Corinthians 1:18, GNB). We all have so many crooked places to be straightened out, so many prejudices and dark corners to be enlightened. When you next hear the word *saved* or *salvation*, I hope you will think of it,

more as a process, rather than a status;

more as life taking on the grand dimensions God intended for it in the beginning;

more as our being brought into greater harmony with ourselves, our neighbours and God.

Sin

THOUGH many today tend to equate *sin* with sexual
irregularities, as did many kirk sessions 200 years ago,
sin in the Bible has much more to do with self-centredness
than sex.

Sin is far more pervasive and radical than that which
we would call immorality. *Sin* is essentially egotism, that
moral twist in life which makes us the centre of the universe,
which pushes away from that centre everything that tries
to impede our freewheeling.

One of the reasons why love of money is, as the Bible
says, the root of all evil, is that it feeds our already swollen
egos. Making 'I' the centre of life, rather than God: that
is sin. Insisting that '*my* will be done,' rather than *God's*
will through me: that is *sin*. Robbery and rape, cheating and
cursing, adultery and arrogance are symptoms of *sin* rather
than the root cause. *Sin* is heart-trouble, not skin disease!

The writer of Genesis reminds us that the root cause
of many of our personal and community problems is that
we human beings have not been content with the role God
has given us in life. In one of the most profound stories
ever written—a story which is eternally, though not literally
true—he tells how Mr and Mrs Everyman succumb to the
temptation to play the role of God, to run the show. They
refuse to acknowledge any law larger than themselves. The
serpent's question, 'Did God really say you shall not eat
of the fruit of the tree?', has many modern versions. Think
of the voices which ask these days, 'Did God really say
you shall not commit adultery?' 'Did God really say you
shall not steal?'

The serpent inferred that it was for one reason only that

the fruit of this singular tree was forbidden. 'Eat and you will be like God.' The temptation is about status—the longing to be the centre of all significance and value, to have the universe come to a focus in us.

Listening to people in the street or at work, we soon become aware how many lives are dominated by the Big 'I': 'My life is my own. Nobody is going to tell me how to behave'—'What's in it for me?'—'You've got to look out for number one!'

An author, proudly extolling his many virtues and achievements, paused momentarily and said: 'But enough of talking about myself. Let's talk about you. What do you think of my latest book?' Of another proud little man who claimed to be self-made, it was rightly said, 'He worshipped his maker.'

Life's critical and constant battle is with this destructive obsession with ourselves. The kind of pride that sets itself at the centre of the universe is the most deadly of sins. It makes its plans and lives its life unmindful of God or what God would have us do with our lives. Recall Mr Dombey in Charles Dickens' novel *Dombey and Son*:

> *Dombey and Son*. These three words conveyed the one idea of Mr Dombey's life. The earth was made for Dombey and son to trade in, and the sun and the moon were made to give them light. Rivers and seas were formed to float their ships; rainbows gave them promise of fair weather; winds blew for or against their enterprise; stars and planets circled in their orbits to preserve inviolate a system of which they were the centre. Common abbreviations took new meanings in his eyes and had sole reference to them. AD had no concern with *Anno Domini*, but stood for *Anno Dombei & Son*.

In the New Testament, one of the most unattractive

characters is the proud Pharisee who, in the temple, extolled his own virtues: 'God, I thank thee that I am not as other men are, extortioners, unjust, adulterers or even as this tax-collector' (Luke 18:11).

Almost as unattractive is the wealthy but totally self-centred farmer. Listen to him talking: 'What shall I do? I have no room to store my goods. This I will do. I will pull down my barns, and build greater. I will do this, that and the other' (Luke 18:17*f*). There is no suggestion in his talking that he was his brother's keeper, or that there was a God to whom he owed primary allegiance.

Pride of rank and wealth, pride of intellect, religious pride—how they detract from life. They blunt our finer sensibilities. They can kill the soul. When Paul said that the wages of sin (egotism) is death, he was stating a basic fact of life. An overgrown love of self, always wanting our own way, is a seeping poison which finally destroys all that is finest in individuals, marriages, families, communities and nations. How often life-enhancing discoveries have been transformed by human egotism into what is deadly.

Self-absorption expresses itself in many forms: greed, irritableness, temper, assertiveness, callousness, hardness, cruelty, prejudice. Think of the pain within families when there is no give and take, when a husband or wife or teenager insists on doing as he or she pleases, with no thought for others. Think of the suffering caused by those whose attitude towards the opposite sex seems to be, 'I love me and want you!'

'I loved to see and choose my path. Pride ruled my will.' The reason why many sing Newman's hymn with such deep feeling is that if we were honest, we would make the same confession.

Wisdom

SOLOMON, in his famous and poignant dream on the night before his accession to the throne (a dream so true to the insights of modern psychology), expressed his fears in a dialogue with God: 'Ask what gift you wish for, and you will have it.' As many of us learned in Sunday school, Solomon did not ask for untold wealth or long life or victory over his enemies. The young man about to be king asked for *wisdom*—'an understanding heart, that I may govern this people justly, and distinguish between good and evil' (1 Kings 3:9). His request was granted. His dream came true. He became WISE—wise in a way that his father David, for all his stature, charisma and gifts had never been. Solomon gained a reputation for *wisdom* that spread over all the inhabited world.

What is *wisdom*? What is this 'understanding heart' for which Solomon wished? Let us approach that question by asking how many people we have known whom we would describe by the epithet *wise*. What is the quality in them that makes us call them that? In our modern culture many might answer that it is the constellation of many qualities: commonsense, intellectual cleverness, unflappability, wealth of experience allied to the ability to think clearly and logically, the ability also to solve problems. Although the Bible has a good deal to say about *wisdom*, it does not focus on any of these things.

Wisdom in the Scriptures is not really an attribute of the MIND. It is a set, a direction, of the HEART. For the Hebrew consciousness, *wisdom* is always moral, ethical, spiritual, rather than academic or aesthetic. So when the embryo King Solomon prayed for an understanding heart, he was not asking that he should never again be baffled by problems, or have the gift of clever utterance which all the world might admire for brilliance. He was asking that his heart be attuned to the will and purpose of God, that he be able to discern the divine dimensions of any situation, the eternal issues involved in local and temporal circumstances.

We have something which our forefathers did not have, to help us grasp the meaning of this prayer of Solomon's. We have a brilliant new translation of the words 'an understanding heart' in the New English Bible : 'Give therefore to thy servant *a heart with skill to listen.*' That is *wisdom.* In our heavily cerebral civilisation, it is important to allow this Hebrew insight to have its way with us.

My own list of wise people contains few who are well-educated, and even fewer who are brilliant and articulate. But all have 'a heart with skill to LISTEN' to their fellow human beings, in an open, transparent, unprejudiced way, compassionately identifying with them. But that description does not exhaust the skill of their listening. All of them seem attuned to a voice that is not human. All seem sensitive to a perspective from beyond. When they speak, they speak out of a depth of listening.

Listening in this Hebrew sense is described as a SKILL. By that is not meant a slick technique that can be mastered by some quick course of counselling or psychotherapy. It is a spiritual gift which, like all other gifts, atrophies when it is not developed and practised.

The willingness to listen is a fundamental prerequisite for those holding authority. When people feel that they are not listened to, but merely legislated for and pontificated to, that their cry, their longings, their dreams are never really heard by those in authority—how can good government take place? What is true for the politician is true all across the board for the professions—the doctor writing his prescription without really listening to the inner story of his patient; the minister haranguing from the pulpit his people who secretly feel he has never bothered to listen to their joys and doubts and fears; the teacher who creates her own gulf between herself and her pupils because, in the air between them, there is the feeling that they don't believe she knows where they are or what they feel—she has not listened.

The following are a few of the elements of this listening which the Bible perceives as *wisdom*:

People who have wisdom listen firstly to themselves. Their ears, their antennae are attuned to 'their own journey' knowing that God speaks through the events of our own lives. The American writer Frederick Buechner in his spiritual classic *The Sacred Journey* helps people find God moving and speaking in the ordinary encounters and events of their own lives. Edwin Muir likewise was convinced that the Passion narrative could only really be heard 'out of' the events of his own life. Recall also Moses' final charge to his people: 'The commandment I command you this day is not too difficult for you, it is not too remote. It is not in heaven ... nor is it beyond the sea .... It is a thing very near you, in your life and in your heart ready to be kept' (Deuteronomy 30.11-14).

A second ingredient of wisdom is the capacity to listen to others, to put oneself aside and stand where others stand, and hear what others are really saying, feel what they are feeling, sense what they are experiencing: so that those others can say, 'Thank God there is someone who really listens to me.'

There is a third dimension to this 'listening skill' which is rising to the fore these days. Those with the skill to listen are listening to the world of Nature, and to the very Earth itself. It is not just to what the birds have to say, or the waves of the sea, as Wordsworth and Keats did; but to the cry of the planet, to its agonies and groans and needs, breaking out in strange ways through strange events.

In the New Testament there is a wonderful cameo of 'listening and non-listening' in the famous story of Martha and Mary. Martha was so commendably busy, all in a good cause. You cannot really bear to find fault with her. But Mary sat at the feet of Jesus and *listened*. That, according to Jesus, was the one thing needful. If we are to have *wisdom* as the Bible thinks of it, we need to do that too, to make time to listen to that special source from which wisdom comes, the record of the life of the wisest Jew of all, Jesus of Nazareth, one who had on his lips 'the wisdom of God,' one whose heart also had the skill to LISTEN.

Word of God

CHRISTIANS commonly use the familiar phrase *Word of God* in the restricted sense of the *Scriptures,* or 'that which comes through to the believer when the Scriptures are read.' 'Hear the *Word of God* as it is written in ....' is the way most readers in Church introduce the Bible passage. A question is left in the mind as to whether the literal words of Scripture (all of them) are equivalent to the Word of God (as if God had dictated them, and no others); or whether the Word of God is something of God's intention and spiritual power which uses the all-too-human words of Scripture as a special vehicle. Those familiar with Church history, both ancient and very recent, will know that this distinction (often loosely described as the Fundamentalist Controversy) has haunted the Church from its earliest days. We ourselves subscribe to the view that the authority of Scripture is the authority of Christ as the heart and soul of Scripture, and that the revelation that comes through the Scriptures is of a unique and special kind, without necessarily implying any literal theory of inspiration.

But the phrase *Word of God* has a far deeper and more interesting genesis. Readers of the Fourth Gospel will be familiar with its striking opening words: 'In the beginning was the Word, and the Word was with God, and the Word was God .... By him all things were made .... In him was life ....' New Testament scholars down the centuries have asked profound questions as to how St John came to use this form of language with such dramatic confidence and authority in the overture to his Gospel. The most dramatic phrase of all, of course, is 'the Word became flesh and dwelt among us .... '

St John inherited a profoundly Jewish way of thinking about God. The Jews had a notion of *Wisdom,* or sometimes *The Law*, as being pre-existently with God before the Creation, and being the source and pervasive power behind all things. There was a large 'Wisdom literature' which complemented the Old Testament in the teaching of the Jewish rabbis. The phrases *Word of God* and *Spirit of God* were sometimes used, but neither of them attained to such authority and prominence as *Wisdom* did. Somehow, in the fermenting period during which the New Testament came to be written, the *Word of God* moved into the centre of the language of revelation, and ousted the concept of *Wisdom.*

The Greeks had a very different notion from the Jews. They held that the structure and unity of the Universe was controlled by REASON and the word they used for REASON was LOGOS (which means *Word*). But it is too simple to say that in taking over this term, St John was simply 'baptising' Jewish ideas into Greek philosophy, making a marriage between them. The whole gospel, from beginning to end, is about Jesus—described as the Truth, the Light, the Life, the Way, the Resurrection, the Door, the Bread which came down from heaven. The whole Gospel is set against the framework of Jewish law (as a counterblast), not in relation to Greek thought. The author did not write his Gospel to prove that Jesus is the Word, but that he is the Christ, the Son of God. One commentator put it this way: 'The workshop in which the Word of God was forged to take its natural place among the great theological descriptions of Jesus and his work is a Christian workshop: the tools are Christian tools.' The evangelist stands under the creative power of the words of Jesus, words that proceed from one source. The figure of Jesus as the embodiment of the glory of the Word of God controls the whole matter of the Christian religion.

So it is in this way that we should understand what lies behind the words which preface the reading of the Scriptures in worship: 'Hear the Word of God.' What we are about to hear is part of the record of the One who is himself the Gospel, the Word of God, and the fulfilment of the Law of God. When the Gospel goes on to say that this Jesus was crucified for our sins, the Greeks (with their passion for intellectual rationality) find the notion a foolishness, while the Jews find it a scandal, an obscenity. But to those who believe, the doctrine of the Cross is the wisdom and the power of a God whose foolishness is wiser than the wisdom of men, and whose weakness is stronger than their strength.

Worship

THE point of including a word like *worship* among the other words in this book is that while for some it may be as natural as breathing, for others it is a bamboozling irrelevance. Anthropologists identify among primitive peoples a sense of awe, a feeling of the 'numinous', a reverence for that which has power over the created order. *Worship* means adoration, veneration; and thus it belongs only to human beings whose frame of reference is 'spiritual' or 'religious'. In a secular society, largely pruned of the sense of the divine, *worship* is in danger of becoming a meaningless word.

You could argue that all human beings worship something. But to compare the adulation paid to rock stars, the eyes lit up with envy and greed at the Motor Show, the mad stampede for shares when a flotation is offered to the public—to compare these things with the meaning of the word *worship* as used by Christians, is to use language which had degenerated beyond recovery. Nearer the mark is the lovely phrase used in certain wedding vows in the Church—'with my body I thee worship'. Anyone who has loved another human being to the point of adoration will understand the sense of reverence that the gift of sexuality implies.

No, worship in its true meaning is *worship of God*. It involves the recognition that the glad response of the whole being, flowing out and spilling over in gratitude, is the natural way for God's children to behave, when they think of his goodness. 'Glory to God in the highest.' Giving God glory, acknowledging his greatness, his love, his kindness, his constancy—telling him this, as his child, because you can do no other—that is the heart of worship.

Two or three difficulties may immediately occur to you, when we claim this meaning for the word. One is that worship, in the Christian Church, has come to be used of 'services of worship' in a building, and has become almost synonymous with that. Hence the complaint sometimes voiced to ministers or elders visiting—'Och, I don't need to go to church to worship. I can do it on the golf course, or in the trout stream—that's far more real for me.' The serious point underneath such an outburst is that Church worship is often seen by the speaker as dull, boring or passive. His true being is not stirred by what is said, sung or done in the House of God on Sunday. The corollary of this is twofold: first, that golf-courses and trout-streams produce a kind of private sense of well-being and appreciation of life's goodness that the speaker is quite happy to call *worship*; and, second, that hymns and prayers and biblical readings telling us what God has done for us in Christ does not evoke for him, that sense of gratitude, reverence and overflow of responsive love that we have claimed for the word *worship*.

Despite this, the Christian Church has always claimed and taught that regular worship was the highest priority for those who seek to follow the way of Jesus. It is the chief 'meaning of grace'; by which is meant that those who keep alive the healthy practice of regular worship will have their faith constantly renewed and refreshed, and will, in some way, be 'brought back to centre'. This last phrase implies that, without worship, we 'lose' the centre: we end up with ourselves, and forget God and his purpose for our life.

The ingredients of worship vary widely across the cultures and nations of the earth, so that a huge diversity arises from various traditions and temperaments across our planet. There is the quiet contemplation of the mystic and the monastic orders; the grave and sacramental liturgy of the

Orthodox, with magnificent chanting and set forms; the privacy of Biblical interpretation in the 'Free' Churches; the humble silent sharing of Quakers—and much more.

But behind, and common to them all is the sense that we need to hear again and again what the Lord God has done, is doing, and promises to do for all of us, saint and sinner, young and old, balanced or baffled or broken. So the 'Word' of the Scriptures is near the heart of all worship, re-telling the shape of the journey of God's people, reminding us of a climactic point when love became one of us in the flesh, and a light shone in the darkness that the darkness can neither understand or extinguish. Singing —a very special human activity of the soul—is a vital part of worship; songs of prayer, or of joy, or of commitment and hope. Prayers, spoken and silent, are natural to worship; as natural as children telling their parents about their experiences, their joys, or their needs. In most Churches there comes a point where words run out and actions take over. The Church calls these sacraments, and they stem from actions of Jesus who taught us to do them to remember him. Worship is usually 'led' by someone taught and trained to try to bring out all its important ingredients. Sometimes the monopoly of this one person over what goes on in worship has been a stumbling-block. Today the 'leading' of worship is increasingly shared between people.

Jesus of Nazareth once said remarkable words to a rather tortured and defensive woman who thought she had the practice of worship quite clear. 'God is a Spirit,' he said to her, 'and they that worship him must worship him in spirit and in truth.' Worship that is just form, and order, and mechanical ritual—which doesn't involve the honesty of the spiritual confrontation with God—is not worship as God wishes from us. Worship, at its best, involves the greatest possibility of miracle, that we should learn to love God again, and turn from our self-centred ways and live.

Part II
TWIN WORDS

SIAMESE twins are often joined in such a way that to try to separate them would mean death for both. In any list of key Christian words there are several pairs of Siamese twins, words and concepts which are mutually dependent on each other. If we separate them, we do irreparable damage to both.

Faith and *Works*

A GENERATION ago Tom Allan and George MacLeod were household names in the Church of Scotland. Tom Allan was the driving force behind the 'Tell Scotland' campaign and the Billy Graham Glasgow Crusade of 1955. Dr MacLeod founded the Iona Community, better to 'Serve Scotland'. He hoped the members of the Community would be a healing influence in the world. Both ministers had a deep faith and a profound social conscience. Although for some people *faith* means little more than the mental acceptance that there is a divine being, for both these men *faith* was 'trust in God.' It was the response of heart, mind and soul to the love of God. Both had dedicated their lives to turning convictions into commitments.

Tom Allan's faith empowered his life: it was personal in its roots, social in its fruits. Through him God breathed new life into two depressed Glasgow churches. He started lunch-time services for those who worked in the city during the day. He and his helpers also offered genuine friendship and a ministry of rehabilitation to those who worked in the city centre at night: the coffee-stall owners and their clients; the prostitutes and theirs.

Few have proclaimed so effectively the power of the Gospel to transform lives as Tom Allan and George MacLeod. Few also have had such a passionate concern for the social implications of the Gospel. For Dr MacLeod, belief in the sovereignty of God meant believing that God has a claim on every area of life, public as well as private, economic and political as well as religious. Throughout his long life he championed the cause of the poor and the oppressed, and those discriminated against. He kept on

challenging the Church to address, in the name of Christ,
such issues as justice, racism, the arms race, war, home-
lessness and unemployment. His concern was for the
whole of life, not just the *holy* bits. Jesus, he said, is Lord
of all or not Lord at all.

Both Tom Allan and George MacLeod stressed the essential unity of *faith* and *works*, of *telling* and *serving*, of
Sunday morning worship and Monday morning work. If
separated, or cut off from each other, if as Dr MacLeod
once said, 'the vertical beam of the Cross is wrenched from
the horizontal, Christianity bleeds.'

It saddened Tom Allan when some of his followers
became so preoccupied with their own private relationship
to God, and saving their own souls, that they failed to relate their new insights and faith horizontally—to create
a more just social order that would reflect God's concern
for the world he so dearly loved. He knew Christian truth
is distorted whenever Christianity is regarded as essentially
other-worldly with little concern for this world. Believing
that God's aim is to redeem this world, to make it a fairer
place for children to be born into, and not just to collect
souls out of it, Tom's concern was as much with discipleship,
as with rebirth. He was as concerned about 'spiritual pe-
diatrics and geriatrics' as about 'spiritual obstetrics.' To
those who rightly rejoiced at having been 'born again,'
at seeing God and life through new eyes, Tom said, 'Fine
but what are you now going to do with your new life?'
He urged the evangelical Christian not only to pray daily,
but also to work daily that God's will might be done on
earth.

He was as concerned with obedience as with grace: 'If
you love me,' said Jesus, 'keep my commandments.' And
though the whole moral appeal of Paul's letter to the
Romans hinges on the grace and goodness of God, the corollary is clear: 'Therefore I implore you by God's mercy

to offer your very selves to him ... to love in all sincerity, cheerfully to help others in distress, to practise hospitality ... to care as much about each other as about yourselves .... ' (Romans 12). The true nature of our faith is revealed when the talking stops and the action starts.

It also saddened Dr MacLeod that some of his followers, who were anxious to solve the world's problems, minimised the importance of worship and personal faith. He knew we are not just social creatures related to one another, but also children of God, related to God. He lived by the faith that behind the struggle for a fairer, more just world, there is a loving, righteous God. It was this faith that under-girded his Christian ideals and put dynamic into his Christian convictions. Social passion by itself has a short life-expectancy. If treading the paths of righteousness is not closely linked with the refreshment that comes from being led by still waters, the glory of the vision can soon fade, the vows can be forgotten, ideals tarnished and as-pirations readjusted. Christian commitment can be likened to running a marathon: fresh, enthusiastic faces as the starting-gun sounds, but along the gruelling way one per-son after another drops out before finishing.

Great living involves intake as well as output, an inner receptivity to a higher world of truth and power. There is a 'fallen' Christianity as well as 'fallen' people, a 'fallen' evangelicalism, which though rightly stressing people's spiritual needs, has minimal concern for what is happening in God's world. The popular hymn 'Amazing Grace' celebrates God's amazing love for unlovely people, but unfortunately has no word about God's claim on our lives.

There is also a fallen liberalism which, though rightly ministering to the physical needs of people, forgets we have deeper hungers, that we do not live by bread alone. Full barns may satisfy cattle, but not people.

The divorce between *faith* and *works* concerned Paul,

John and James centuries before. 'If I have faith strong
enough to move mountains, but have not love, it profiteth
me nothing.' 'Love must not be a matter of words and talk.
It must be genuine and show itself in action.' 'What use
is it for a man to say he has faith when he does nothing
to show it? …. If faith does not lead to action it is a lifeless
thing …. Faith divorced from deeds is barren.'

When the Roman Empire was disintegrating, St Jerome, one of the great biblical scholars of the early Church,
was running a monastery in Bethlehem. To escape the
barbarous hordes, refugees came pouring into the Holy
Land. Writing of this time, Jerome said, 'The crowds of
homeless made me want to turn the words of scripture into
deeds, not just saying holy things but doing them.'

Are we in our day following Jesus or simply believing
in Christ? Some Churches get more worked up about theological heresies such as second baptism, than ethical
heresies such as members harbouring racial prejudices,
or grudges against those who wrong them. Is there an imbalance in the questions put to new communicants, and
those being ordained? Is the emphasis more on the acceptance
of certain treasured beliefs about God and Jesus, the inspiration of the Bible, and a certain form of Church
government, than on *following Jesus*.

Yet read the Gospels and you will probably find Jesus
asking someone to follow him. The Greek verb meaning
to follow is found 80 times. As well as revealing the nature
of God, Jesus also revealed the nature of sonship and discipleship. Studying a guide book and accepting the
information in it, is no substitute for making the journey.

Some in the Church today say that evangelism is *the*
priority, others that *the* priority is making ours a more caring
society: in fact both are vitally important. People need a *faith*
to guide them and to hold on to. People also need caring
love. As a Church we are called both to *tell* and *serve*.

Freedom and *Responsibility*

THE biblical story is about God's struggle to set people free—sometimes from bondage, sometimes from their enemies, sometimes from their lower natures. The theme of *freedom* is so central to the New Testament that one could in fact describe its essential message as 'The Gospel of *Freedom.*' Jesus said, 'You shall know the truth and the truth shall make you *free*' (John 8:32). Writing to the Corinthians Paul said, 'Where the Spirit of the Lord is, there is *freedom*' (2 Cor 3:17). To the Romans he spoke of the 'glorious liberty of the children of God' (8:21). To the Galatians he said, 'You my friends were called to be free men, only do not turn your *freedom* into licence for your lower nature, but be servants to one another in love' (5:13, NEB).

Freedom is a volcanic idea, capable of setting whole continents aflame with revolution. It is also a very misunderstood idea. Some equate freedom with doing what they want, where and when they want, with the removal of all physical and moral controls. It concerned Paul that some of the Galatians were using their new found freedom not to serve one another in love, but for riotous living. When freedom is divorced from *responsibility* and a respect for law, it can go desperately wrong. One of the saddest chapters in Jewish history was when each person did what 'was right in his own eyes' (Judges 17:6).

When Moses said to Pharaoh, 'Let my people go', his dream of liberty was no cheap notion of release from all restraint and authority. He wanted freedom for his people that they might serve God more faithfully. No sooner had he released them from the authority of Pharaoh, than he

confronted them with the authority of God's commandments. Centuries later, the freedom Paul proclaimed was
not freedom from the content of the moral law, but freedom
from the legalistic outlook, from the innumerable rules
and regulations covering almost every area of human experience—the Sabbath, circumcision, fasting, diet, and the
offering of animal sacrifices. For Paul the glorious thing
about Christianity was that it freed people from preoccupation
with such petty rules and rituals, and from the necessity
of performing certain spiritual gymnastics to gain God's
favour.

Freedom, as Paul conceived it, is a precious commodity,
but unless accompanied by responsibility, and a worthwhile
goal, it is a questionable boon. People's worst difficulties
often begin when they are able to do as they please, when
they are freed from external authority. The temptation is
strong to swing the pendulum to the other extreme. Because some of the early Christians had done just that, Paul
was forced to write, 'Do not turn your freedom into licence
for your lower nature .... ' I am sure we can all think of
young people reared in fine homes who went to pieces
during college years, when they were free to do as they
wanted. They could not handle their new found freedom.
It is often the same with those who win or are left a small
fortune. For the first time they have money to buy what
they like. Unfortunately they often turn their new financial
freedom into licence for their lower nature.

One reason why newly-won freedom is so often accompanied by excess and irresponsibility is that many people
misunderstand freedom. They think of it as being more
from something, rather than *for* something. Whereas today,
to be free means to be independent, in ancient times to be
free, a *freeman*, meant having a real share in, and responsibility for, the ongoing life and work of the state. In the
New Testament, Christian freedom is conceived in terms

of being free to shoulder responsibilities, free, as Paul says, 'to be servants to one another in love.'

Abraham Lincoln, one of the greatest champions of human liberty, used the word *responsibility* almost as often as he used the word *freedom*. In our own day no one has been more aware of the importance of freedom than Vaclav Havel, the President of Czechoslovakia. Yet in a letter which he wrote from prison to his wife, he said, 'Responsibility is the mortar which holds society together.'

Freedom in the physical world is always within limits, and it is a blessing it is so. We are not free to walk through a brick wall, or see through it. The law of gravity severely restricts the height we can jump, the distance we can drive a golf ball. But there is a credit side to such limitations. Because we cannot see or walk through walls, neither can others. There can thus be such a thing as privacy. And although the law of gravity curtails how far we can propel a ball, it is that restricting law which makes games like football, tennis and golf possible. We are free to fly from the earth's surface, but we are not free from the laws of aerodynamics. If at any moment the conditions governing such flights are no longer satisfied, the flight will stop abruptly.

The scientist's concern being for truth, he has a responsibility to truth. The artist's concern being for beauty, he has a responsibility to beauty. They are servants of truth and beauty respectively. This limits their freedom. The Christian's first love is for God as made known in Jesus, and consequently his prime responsibility is to God. Such love and responsibility have kept many from becoming slaves to their ambitions or passions. What galling slaveries these can be. The person who is mastered by the desire for money or applause or drink is the most pitiable of all captives.

As a boy, Michelangelo wanted to be free to be an artist, but his family had other ideas. When he so much as spoke of art, they beat him. Finally he left his imprisoning home, saying in effect, 'Now all the world belongs to me and I belong to beauty.' At least in the realm of art, his freedom was safe. True liberty comprises freedom and loyalty, freedom and responsibility. In some parts of the world loyalty is demanded but no real freedom granted. In other parts, where freedom is unaccompanied by responsibility, the result is just as frightening. In the West the words 'obedience' and 'self-discipline' are not in favour. The in-words are 'freedom' and 'individualism.' In their search for happiness, thousands are loyal neither to God, employers, spouses, parents or anyone else. The horizon of their concern does not extend beyond fulfiling their own desires, and exploring the borderland around the old rules.

Once, on a ship whose rudder had broken off in a wild sea, a woman sought to console the captain: 'Never mind, it was down where nobody could see it. It won't make much difference.' It makes as little sense to minimise the importance of loyalty and responsibility. A ship without a rudder is in one sense more free than one under the control of a helmsman. But as it veers with every wind that blows and threatens to turn over with every sudden squall, it is a travesty of real freedom. A ship is most free when controlled by her captain.

Consider another illustration. If there are no banks to contain a river, it will simply make a bog. But if the river is enclosed in a suitable channel, it will drive a mill or a dynamo. Likewise when a person's desires and emotions are unified and given direction by their love for Christ and the things for which Christ stood, the narrow path becomes a roomier place than the broad way of unlimited freedom.

In his first sermon at Nazareth, Jesus announced that he had come to set the captives free. To that end the first thing he did was to bind them to himself: 'Follow me and I will make you .... '—that reveals the paradox of

Christian freedom. We are never really free until bound voluntarily by a higher loyalty.

Jane Welsh, later to become Mrs Thomas Carlyle, tells how at the age of nine, she idealised the Romans. When reading about them, she fell in love with their heroic and masterful qualities. If she wanted to prevent herself acting in a selfish or cowardly manner, she would say 'a Roman would not do this.' Likewise the Christian is not free to do things which Christ would not approve of.

Great conduct moves in the realm of obligations which cannot be enforced by law. No slave-driver could have extracted by force from Mother Teresa a fraction of what she has willingly done because of her love of Christ and underprivileged people. No Roman Emperor could have made St Paul tramp for twenty years across Europe and Asia, enduring hardship and persecution. Paul speaks for them both when he says, 'The love of Christ constraineth us' (2 Corinthians 5:14). Love and loyalty can achieve what no law can accomplish.

How much more attractive is a life lived for others to the glory of God than a life that is primarily concerned with making no mistakes and breaking no laws. How much more attractive is the oratorio than the most flawless playing of scales. Dr George Buttrick once said of Fritz Kreisler, the famous violinist, 'We cannot see and hear him without seeing a flame burning on the high altar. But he is not free from the musical laws. He is free in the law, so gloriously free that he can make wood, glue, silk strands and cat-gut sing like a choir of angels.' Jesus was likewise free to be loyal to his Father. At the end, with his own battered body for a violin, and a cross for the bow, he made undying music.

Judgment and *Mercy*

ON summer evenings when the Dornoch pipe band parades in the Cathedral Square, I can often hear their music in my study half a mile away. But sometimes, depending on wind direction, all I hear is the pounding of the big drums.

From earliest times there have been those in the Church who in their theology have heard only the deep rumbling of divine *judgment*. Some became hell, fire and thunder preachers. Such, early on, was the writer of the Apocalypse of 1 Peter. This book was written about AD 130. It was falsely made out to be a revelation given to Peter in which he was supposedly furnished with inside information about life after death. The writer delights in gory descriptions of hell. 'And other men and women were being burned up to their middle and cast down into a dark place, and scourged by evil spirits, and having their entrails devoured by worms ....' Dante's gruesome descriptions of hell were based on this Apocalypse. I am convinced it was divine wisdom that prompted the Western and Syrian Churches to dismiss this Apocalypse from their New Testament.

In the Church where Martin Luther worshipped as a boy, Jesus was portrayed in stained glass as coming with a drawn sword to judge the wicked. That picture of Christ the All-terrible, long remained uppermost in Luther's mind. He heard only the deep rumbling of the wrath of God. Even though his fellow monks regarded him as a model of piety, Luther was certain he was an outcast from God and 'gallows ripe.'

Two hundred years later Jonathan Edwards, the distinguished Puritan preacher, in his infamous sermon, 'Sinners in the hands of an angry God', said: 'The God that holds you over the pit of hell abhors you .... His wrath towards you burns like fire .... ' During this supposedly 'Christian' sermon, we are told that one worshipper finally interjected, 'But Mr Edwards, is not God also a gracious God?' The noteworthy thing is that Edwards often preached on the *mercy* and love of God. The imbalance was created by his keeping the judgment and mercy of God in two separate compartments. To think of God as an ill-tempered Eastern caliph or a spiteful judge, sitting with judgment books ever open, books in which are recorded every action and word that anyone has ever said or done, or as a monster detective delighting in collecting incriminating evidence, is to misrepresent God. It is to forget what Jesus and the Psalmist taught, that God is kindly disposed towards us, and 'plenteous in mercy'.

The other extreme is also sub-Christian—thinking of God only as a tender shepherd. Modern liberalism has often eradicated the drum beat, concentrating on the more appealing pibroch music. The emphasis in our day is on the love of God, rather than the wrath of God. Though we can never talk too *much* about the loving kindness and tender mercy of God, we can speak about them too *exclusively*, and in a way that takes no account of judgment. Having understandably rejected the cruder pictures of hell, some have in the process also discarded the reality of God's hatred of sin. They think of God as Maeterlinck did, as a grandfather in heaven, 'sitting on a sunny mountain smiling at our gravest offences as only the naughtiness of puppies playing on the hearth-rug.' I sometimes wonder if part of the appeal of spiritualism is that it contains no idea of God as judge.

The Bible never portrays God as a doting grandparent who makes light of our self-centredness, apathy or shortcomings, or smooths them over with a benevolent tut-tut. The God of Abraham, the Psalmist and Jesus do not betray love with a kiss. I get angry when I hear of children being abused, or see women selling their bodies to men on the look-out for a bargain, or when I hear of drug-dealers selling their damaging product to depressed teenagers. The phrase 'the wrath of God' is a reminder that it is no different with God. Like every good and loving father, God is uncompromisingly opposed to whatever corrupts or threatens to harm the children he loves. It is surely not surprising that there is an equivalent of this kind of anger in our heavenly Father. Malachi says, 'You have wearied the Lord ... by saying that all evil-doers are good in the eyes of the Lord, that he is pleased with them' (Malachi 2:17, NEB). He then lists some of the things that make God angry: marital unfaithfulness, with all the consequent trauma inflicted on children; false testimony; cheating employees out of fair wages; taking advantage of widows, orphans or foreigners, and so on.

What a commentary Christ's death was on the length, breadth and height of God's love, and his incredible mercy; yet what tremendous judgment too on human pride and selfishness. To take the element of judgment out of the Cross is to take the nerve out of the Gospel. *Mercy* and *judgment* are two inseparable aspects of God's love, two sides of the one coin. God is both judge and redeemer. The tragedy is that often in Christian history we have separated them with alarming consequences.

One day the vicar-general of the monastery in which Luther was living, realising the mental anguish which Luther was passing through, suggested that he should study the Scriptures. Little did he realise the change in the life of Luther and the life of the Church that this would bring about. The more we study Christ's life and teaching, the more we realise that love, as Jesus understood it, contains not only what people call *mercy*, but what they call *judgment*. In Christ's dealings with people, what at first appears to be judgment is ultimately seen to be mercy, and what appears to be mercy contains the element of judgment.

In Graf Harrach's painting of the denial of Christ, the cock has just crowed. Peter hangs his head in shame. Jesus, passing by, turns and looks at Peter. It is a disappointed look. He is saddened that his best friend has denied him, but he still loves Peter. A maid carrying a pitcher of water is pointing at Peter. The soldiers are jeering at him. But neither the pointing finger, nor the mocking, hurt Peter nearly as much as Jesus' merciful and forgiving look. That was the greatest judgment. The big fisherman went out and cried like a child. Later by the lakeside, when the Risen Christ said to Peter, 'Do you love me?', was it judgment or mercy?

In the Zaccheus story, Jesus did not say, 'Zaccheus you are a sinner, a cheat, a fraud. Only if you admit it will I come and dine with you.' It was in fact only when Zaccheus knew that, despite his past, he was accepted and forgiven, that he repented, confessed his shortcomings and sought to make reparation. Was Jesus' going to Zaccheus' house, judgment or mercy? Were they not the two inseparable aspects of Jesus' concern for the person Zaccheus could yet become?

Recall also the tenderness, yet firmness of Christ's remark to Judas when he brought the soldiers, 'Friend, why have you come?' Was it judgment or mercy? Judas went out and hanged himself. The mercy was too great a judgment. Again, how awful it must have been for the woman taken in adultery to come face to face with Jesus who radiated purity and compassion. 'Go your way and sin no more.' Was it judgment or mercy?

The greatest *judgment* is often to be treated better than we deserve: yet isn't that also *mercy*?

Justification and *Sanctification*

MOST human beings have a sense that all is not well with themselves and their world. In some, this apprehension is so highly developed that they become deeply fixated with guilt. Others hardly give the matter a passing thought; or they discuss the pressure upon their conscience with some easy formula: 'Well, we're all human, aren't we?' Agnostics and atheists, as well as believing Christians, have somehow to account for the existence of evil. Two appalling World Wars, the remorselessness of human tragedy and suffering, the rising statistics of crime, make quite impossible some glib view that Utopia is possible and that human nature is changing for the better.

The most important starting-point, as in most things, is an accurate diagnosis of what is wrong with the human condition. There are many who feel that the Christian diagnosis is lamentably pessimistic. They believe that suffering and evil can be ameliorated by social engineering, better education, proper global political management or financial restructuring. The Christian claim is that the human 'illness' is fundamental, deep and all-pervasive. We are 'out of relation' with God, deeply alienated from him and from each other, in a condition so drastic that the only remedy lies in God's hands. We need to be redeemed. We stand in the wrong, unrighteous and unholy, unable to put ourselves right. Christians call this condition 'sin.'

How on earth can we be put right? What could God do to bridge the gulf between himself and those whom he created to be his true children, but who had flung themselves away from him in their sinfulness? The Jewish people had a tremendous sense that God was calling them to be

a Holy Nation, different from the nations who surrounded
them, obedient to a word and a will that kept asking them
to turn from wickedness and live. When this vision, this
pressure, faded—as it frequently did—figures whom they
called prophets rose up among them to do the unpopular
job of recalling the nation to fundamentals. But the prophets were not heeded and things went from bad to worse.

The teaching of the Church is that God entered this
closed circle, this awful situation, himself. He became
born into poverty as a man—Jesus of Nazareth—without
ceasing to be God the Creator of all. Jesus lived as no other
has been able to live, a life of utter self-giving and loving
identification with his fellow human beings. This inevitably involved suffering and hideous condemnation by
those with vested interests in politics and religion. His truth
confronted their lies, his goodness their evil, just by being
what it was— a clean light in a dark world. He died in ex-
cruciating aloneness upon a criminal's gallows, aged
perhaps thirty-three.

Christians believe that the key to the healing of the
world's evil, viciousness, suffering and sin is to be found
in that place, on that Cross, in that figure. By living as he
lived, by loving as he loved, by dying as he died, Jesus
bore in himself the sufferings and sins of all human beings
—those who believed in him and those who rejected him.
More than this, it became clear that God 'vindicated' Jesus,
and raised him from death. The meaning of this is very
wonderful, and we can only grasp fringes of it. Part of the
meaning is that our sinful human condition has been dealt
with, once and for all, in a great transaction and 'exchange'
on that execution hill.

So Christians believe that we have, through no merit
or goodness of our own, been 'put in the right' with God
through Jesus's life and death. The whole thing from beginning to end is the gift of God, and Christians call this

gift 'grace'. In no other way could the restoration, the reconciliation happen. Luther, following St Paul, broke through to the utterly miraculous nature of this truth with his great teaching on justification by faith alone. The word 'alone' is meant to exclude all thought of sinful man's 'earning' or 'deserving' justification by good works. The believer is, first and foremost, asked to accept as utter miracle what the Gospel tells him has happened: that Jesus has stood in the place he should have occupied—the criminal's dock—and taken upon himself the punishment.

Now that great happening—our salvation—does not mean that what we do, or how we live, is unimportant. To be justified through faith in God's sheer grace puts us into a new relationship of love, gratitude and obligation to our Father God, just as the prodigal son's behaviour was never to be the same after his wonderful and utterly unexpected welcome home. This is where the Christian teaching on *sanctification* follows as a close corollary to the teaching on *justification*.

We have been 'put in the right.' Now we have to live in a new way, bearing the fruits of the knowledge that we have been liberated from the burden of our guilt and sin. We are asked to be holy: that is, to try to share in the very life of God.

The Church provides the means by which we can do this, through the sacraments, and through its preaching of the Gospel. We are to accept that we are children of God, freely redeemed, and begin to live in the light of it. No works that we can do—works of mercy or piety (to use Wesley's terms)— can alter the fact that God puts us 'in the right' with him by grace alone through faith alone. Graces of character, a capacity to love God and our neighbour better, are not achievements upon which we may rest in satisfaction. Any loveliness in our life is hideously unlovely compared with the loveliness of the holiness of God.

But the Christian, who has been forgiven and restored by the goodness of God, is asked to try to grow in goodness, and is encouraged to expect wholesome change in his or her life. This will happen if the Christian tries to live by the example of Jesus, and shares in the very life of Jesus through the sacrament of Holy Communion which Jesus gave to nourish us. It becomes, as our forebears said, a 'means of grace.' St Paul, in the first chapter of Romans, addresses ordinary sinful people with the dramatic words 'you, who are called to be Saints.' There is no false piety in the phrase—just the magnificent recognition that because of what Christ has done for us, we had better get on with the business of living as God intended us to live.

Mind and *Soul*

LADY Astor told a story of a minister who was recounting in his vivid way the Creation Story: 'Once there was nobody in the world, wasn't white folks or black folks. God was lonely. So he got some mud and stood it up against a fence to dry, and breathed on it, and made it into a man, and that was the beginning of the world.' Just then a little boy's voice asked, 'Mr Preacher, if that was the beginning of the world, who made the fence?' 'Child,' said the preacher, 'It's questions like that what's just ruining religion.'

I could not disagree more. Asking questions has purged my faith of much dross, making it far more vital. During science studies at university, I used to feel that of all Jesus' commands, the one least observed by his followers was to love God with all our minds. In some Churches and many homes, including my own, free-thinking and the questioning of religious beliefs were discouraged. As a teenager it concerned me where Cain got his wife from, and how there could be light on the earth three days before God created the sun and stars. And yet it was by seriously asking such questions that I was led to a deeper understanding of what the Bible essentially is: not a scientific text book about how the world was created or how life developed on it, but a book that introduces us to the Wisdom, Love and Power behind all created things. The writers of Genesis were no more concerned with physics, geology or astronomy than Burns was concerned with botany when he wrote, 'My love is like a red, red rose.' Their concern was with ultimate questions, the purposes of God, the meaning of life, and what had gone wrong with the human situation.

The anti-intellectualism in some Churches, the inherent

suspicion of philosophers and scientists, the exiling of the word 'doubt' to religion's semantic dog-house, continues to sadden me, for the human *mind* with its ability to analyse, question and think God's thoughts after him, is one of God's greatest gifts. Jesus questioned many of the beliefs of his day, the belief about a military-type Messiah who would put an end to Roman occupation, the belief that Samaritans were an inferior race, and that the true law was 'an eye for an eye and a tooth for a tooth.'

Faith can benefit from the doubt. The Christian faith has nothing to fear from the honest search after truth. Down through the centuries some of the wisest and most brilliant intellects have professed faith in Christ: Paul, Augustine, Dostoevsky, C S Lewis and Solzhenitsyn, for instance. Faith is the stronger for being informed by intelligence. The failure of many church members to love the Lord their God with all their *mind*, saddens me. A bit of Christian education in childhood is too often followed by creeping illiteracy.

The Church also suffers from a reluctance on the part of many outside the Church to seek meaningful answers to life's greatest questions. During a group discussion a young man said, 'I would give anything to believe in God?' 'Would you really,' said a wise old man. 'How long is it since you read a book that might have helped clarify your understanding of God. How long is it also since you sought out someone who might have helped you believe in God? The student had to admit that he had done neither. Yet he would have done anything to believe in God!

Church services short-change the listener if they do not minister to the thinking side of the brain, but they also short-change the worshipper if they do not minister to the 'silent,' visual side. John Calvin and the Puritans rightly stressed the importance of the word of God being heard in worship services, but unfortunately often starved the worshippers of visual and emotional uplift. They forgot there is a holiness about harmony and beauty, as well as a beauty about holiness. There was no place for bright and beautiful things in their stark churches. Nothing was allowed to detract from the true beauty of God's word. The Orcadian poet Edwin Muir, wrote of the services of his childhood, the lengthy prayers and sermons: 'There the Word made flesh is made word again.'

More than the cold prose of ordinary speech is needed to do justice to the glory and wonder of the Christian faith. Great music, rousing hymns, a lovely sanctuary, meaningful symbols, these can all help. A faith that by-passes the emotions will not ultimately satisfy the human *soul*. Hebrew psychology saw the soul as the seat of the emotional life. We display emotion in our love of family and country, why not in our worship? I believe worship should help people live from the neck down, as well as the neck up.

Religious purists are often critical of 'heart-words' and 'heart-music.' They forget the real educators are the storytellers. They will have nothing to do with 'gospel' hymns that affect people mainly at an emotional level; or any hymn that emphasises the word 'I' or 'my' instead of the objective glory of God. I am also critical of some of these hymns. The theology sometimes leaves much to be desired; but I am also aware it is good theology to be aware that God is not dependent on good theology. Some of the Kirk's finest ministers and members grew up in churches, and were influenced by crusades, where the emphasis in the hymns and preaching was on a theology they would now reject. God has often spoken through poor theology and not so great hymns.

Without heart and soul, Christian orthodoxy lacks warmth. Without mind, the religion of the heart can easily become irrational and over sentimental. Passion needs to be united with reason, *mind* with *soul*.

Mission and *Evangelism*

THE word *evangel* means 'good news'. Whereas all members of the early Church thought of themselves as evangelists, bearers of good news about a God who is kindly disposed towards us, for the majority of us today, the words *mission* and *evangelism* are associated with the few rather than the many.

As a boy my image of missionaries was of a few dedicated people who went out, Bible in hand, to foreign lands. Fifty years later the image many have of evangelists is that of a few preachers of world-renown calling on people at mass rallies to come forward and accept Christ as their Saviour. Others associate the word *evangelism* with a few pushy people who accost strangers and effectively ask where they intend to spend eternity. Commenting on this aggressive approach to evangelism, Dr Andrew Herron said, 'The evangel is as wide and welcoming as some evangelists would have it narrow and forbidding ... I find it difficult to apply the term *evangel*—glad tidings—to the news that most of us are destined for the nether regions.'

Within the Church there are those who claim for themselves a monopoly on evangelism, people who are big in religious language, who constantly verbalise what Jesus is doing in their lives, and sometimes to such an extent that it is difficult to get to know them as human beings. Those who belong to 'evangelical Churches' put more stress on public witness than those belonging to more liberal Churches. Evangelicals believe this is because they have got hold of the right end of the stick, but I sometimes wonder whether there is not a close relation between a rather mechanically conceived faith and a stereotyped pattern of evangelism. What sometimes passes under the name of evangelism and mission is a travesty of what Christian *evangelism* and *mission* are really all about.

The whole concept of mission and evangelism has been bedevilled by the Church regarding the laity as a lower form of ecclesiastical life than the clergy. We talk today of the 'role of the laity,' a strange phrase considering that the laity constitute at least 98 per cent of the Church. Lay people immersed in the life of the world are the real agents of mission.

The driving force for evangelism is not first and foremost to get more Church members, even though that would be a bonus. It is the desire to share with others, for their well-being, a faith that we have found to be life-enriching; and also the desire to help people live together in love. Christians are called to be salt to the earth, remembering always that the purpose of salt is not to turn everything it touches into salt, nor to remain safely in a container where it is indistinguishable from sugar. Salt fulfils its function when it adds flavour to its environment.

Likewise the primary aim of evangelism is not religiousness, but the enlarging and enriching of life—making people more fully human. The offer of genuine authentic life is at the heart of the Christian faith. 'Go and speak to the people and tell them about this new life and all that it means.' To people no worse and no better than you and me, Jesus said, 'I am come that you might have life and have it more abundantly.' The wealth that the Church seeks to share is *life*.

The best evangelists are those radiant personalities who have a great deal of love in their hearts, who witness by their comradeship, their conscientious workmanship, their caring and forgiving attitude. It is a real bonus if, in the light of our Christian faith in the Jesus-likeness of God, we are able to interpret for others the deeper meaning of everyday experiences. In the hearts of many there is a strong but muddled religious feeling. The Church has a major educational and evangelistic task if some of this latent feeling is to be translated into a more articulate and conscious belief and practice. Being an Interpreter is an integral part of being an Evangelist. Whereas many equate religious experience with some uncanny or spine-tingling experience, far more often it is normal experience understood at greater depth

H A Williams, who exerted such a profound influence on the religious thought of Prince Charles, has written:

My deepest feelings told me that what I ought to do was to get to know people, to establish with them relations of confidence to whatever degree was possible, and thus perhaps be invited by them to share their joys and sorrows, problems and aspirations. It was in that communion with them, I felt that God's real presence was to be found, not in trying to sell God to people as if he were a patent medicine, with the Church as the chemist's shop where it could be obtained. Yet God as a universal patent medicine had been so drummed into me both from my earliest years at home and during my training at Cuddesdon [theological college] that I felt horribly guilty by my own lack of desire to make people technically religious.

Evangelism involves making human contact with people before religious contact. To begin with it involves praying *for* people rather than *with* them. In some Churches the pressure is considerable for the members to affirm publicly the 'brand theology' of that Church: what they imagine they should as Christians be saying. That pressure has to be resisted. If, in speaking about what our faith means to us, we have to choose between words that mean more than our experience and words that mean less, I believe we should choose the words that mean less. That way we leave room for our hearers to move around in, and for ourselves to move around in. It is better to understate than overstate.

In evangelism the role of those closest to young people in their early years is crucial. Dr Bill Coffin speaks of the influence of his Swiss governess Mademoiselle Lovey:

> Her plain face shone with a kindness that radiated through every pore. From her I absorbed not only French, but most of the religious piety that was not mine by inheritance. She and I took everything to God in prayer, from the simple beauty of a day, to the tears we shed when the newspapers announced that the kidnapped Lindbergh baby had been found dead. To this day it is still easier for me to say the Lord's prayer in French, a reflection of the fact that my greatest childhood intimacy was with Mlle Lovey and God.

If, on the other hand, those closest to children seldom speak of God and do not attend Church, it is unlikely that the children will have a meaningful Christian faith or a strong Church connection.

Though evangelism and mission may have become discredited words, at their finest they stand for something absolutely basic and necessary in the life of the Church. The faith is never more than two generations from extinction! Christianity never has been spread and never will be spread by a vagueness of belief. Too many Church members, who in other areas of their lives—politics, the arts, education, child rearing *etc*—can give a good intelligent account of where they stand, flounder in confused silence about matters relating to faith. We desperately need Christians who, because they have made time to study and clarify what they believe, are able with quiet sensitivity to share their spiritual insights, and are not afraid to expose themselves to the sharp questions of those who don't share their Christian beliefs.

The Church has been entrusted with a great shining torch. We are to pass it on in the hope that succeeding generations will do better with it than we have done.

Predestination and *Free-will*

IN July 1990, 1400 pilgrims died in a tunnel near Mecca. They were suffocated and trampled to death in a frantic bid to escape after a power failure had cut off the air supply. Commenting on this appalling accident, the King of Saudi Arabia said it was predestined that they should die. If they had not died in that tunnel, he said, they would have died somewhere else at the same time. That kind of remark degrades the whole idea of providence and *predestination*. I would find it impossible to worship a God who deliberately decreed such awful happenings.

In our own country there are also those who believe that we are simply actors in a divine drama, all the scenes and words of which have been written out in full. 'What will be will be,' they say; 'what's for us will not go past us.'

Such a fatalistic outlook sometimes stems from a feeling of personal helplessness. People become convinced that life is turning out the way it is because they were born under a certain star or because it was all so decreed. Freedom of choice is regarded as an illusion. They believe that what happens at every moment was determined by God when, in the beginning, he wrote the great script in every detail. By such a fatalistic outlook we are nothing more than puppets mechanically doing what God has predestined. One of the best comments on this is Maurice Hare's limerick:

There once was a man who said 'Damn!
It is borne in upon me that I am
An engine that moves
In predestinate grooves
I'm not even a bus, I'm a tram.'

Perhaps God could have thus chosen to express his sovereignty, but I am perfectly certain he did not so choose.

'What will be will be': how far removed such an outlook is from the teaching of Jesus. He did not always identify what happened with the will of God. He cured the sick, and restored sight to the blind. He did not regard these afflictions as the will of God.

Central to biblical thought is the belief that we have *free-will*. As the writer of the ancient Epistle to Diognetus said, 'Coercion is not an attribute of God.' We are free to accept or reject God. We are free to create heaven or hell on earth. God risked a very great deal in giving us this freedom to rebel. Instead of destroying those who do so—mark you they often finish up destroying themselves and their world—God goes on loving and appealing, working behind the scenes, hoping that one day they might love and serve in return.

Common sense is on the side of biblical theology. The assurance that as human beings we are free and responsible for what we do, underlies not only Christianity, but any authentic concept of human life.

Though environment and heredity do influence us and determine many of the temptations to which we are subject, they do not victimise us. We are not corks tossing helplessly in a strong current that we have no power to resist. We all have the power to say 'no'. Is not the reason we often regret what we do or say, because deep down we know it was not predetermined that we should behave the way we did? The reason many are weighed down with worry is because they have constantly to make important decisions. If choice is ultimately an illusion, then we would have to conclude that our feelings completely deceive us. During a learned discussion on predestination and free-will, Dr Samuel Johnson was heard to interject, 'We know our will is free and there is an end of it.' On this occasion I can sympathise with the abruptness of the eminent doctor.

In the minds of many, the doctrine of predestination is closely linked with John Calvin. Calvin believed that everything was determined in the beginning by God's inscrutable will. I often wonder how much Calvin's own temperament influenced his theological thought. He was a born organiser. He himself was not happy unless everything was arranged to the last detail. 'God has decreed by his eternal and immutable counsel those whom he willed to take for salvation, and those whom he willed to devote to perdition.' John Milton called Calvin's God a tyrant. Burns also hit hard at this awful doctrine in his poem, 'Holy Willie's Prayer':

> *O thou that in the heavens does dwell*
> *Wha as it pleases best Thysel*
> *Sends ane to heaven and ten to Hell*
> *A' for Thy glory*
> *And no for any guid or ill*
> *They've done before Thee.*

I believe it was because Calvin separated the doctrine of predestination from Christ that he reached such woeful conclusions. A God who sends people to hell just for his glory is not the God revealed to the world in Jesus.

In his letter to the Romans, Paul attempts to fathom the mystery of the relationship between the providence of God and our free-will. Finally he gives up. His attempt at systematic theology turns to poetry. 'How unsearchable are God's judgments, how untraceable his ways.'

The doctrine of predestination reminds us of certain great truths. It says something important about God's ultimate purpose for us. Writing to the Romans, Paul says we are predestined 'to be conformed to the image of God's son' (Romans 8:29). Writing to the Ephesians, he said, 'we are destined in love to be God's sons' (Ephesians 1:4, 5). In other words, what God predestined was not that we should be suffocated in a tunnel at a certain moment, or catch pneumonia on a particular day, or fall in love on a certain night—but that we should become more conformed to Christ's image, more filled with his Spirit, more open to his guidance, more willing to allow him to do for us what we cannot do for ourselves. This was God's great intention for us.

The doctrine of predestination also reminds us that we all have a part to play in the drama of history—*His*-story. Though the parts are not written out in full, God has given us sufficient light to know the aim and object of life, sufficient clue to the meaning of the great drama in which he wants us to co-operate. The Bible is 'a lantern for our feet and a light for our paths,' not an oracle that tells us exactly what lies ahead of us. We are free to chose the paths of righteousness or more selfish paths. We are free to accept or reject God's purpose and guidance.

Picture children playing beside a tiny stream that runs down a mountainside to join the river below. The children can divert the stream by damming it with stones and earth. But they cannot prevent the water reaching its goal at last. Likewise, belief in predestination reminds us that in a world in which we have power to work havoc, to make awful mistakes, the final purposes of God will not be defeated. He remains master of the situation, and we remain free.

Another clue to understanding predestination is to be found in the analogy of falling in love. We do not fall in love simply by making up our mind that we are going to do so. Falling in love is our response to something in the life of another that reaches out and elicits love from us. We are not forced into falling in love. In fact we are never so free as when we do the will of the person we love. Predestination is the Bible's way of saying that the initiative

in loving is God's, that God loved us before we got ourselves round to loving him. If we respond to him in love
we will find our true destiny. If we say 'no' we will miss
our true destiny.

The fatalistic belief is that life simply involves waiting
to find out what God has already decreed for us. It denies
human freedom and responsibility. It makes us puppets,
rather than persons. Predestination concerns rather God's
hope for each one of us that instead of living self-centred
lives we will grow in Christ-like goodness, graciousness
and humility, and use the talents he has given us to enrich
the life of his world, to help with that particular fragment
of God's plan and purpose that is within our power and
range.

Truth and *Love*

I HAVE forgotten most of the chemistry I learned at school, but I do remember that sodium is a very active element that has to be kept in a special container.

I also remember that chlorine is a poisonous gas with an unattractive smell. When these two substances combine they form sodium chloride, the common salt which adds flavour to food.

That seems to me to be a kind of parable. When *truth* and *love*, the spiritual equivalents of sodium and chlorine, go hand in hand, we have what Jesus wanted—people who are the salt of the earth. But separate them and you have all kinds of problems, and problem people.

'By this shall all men know that you are my disciples, if you love one another.' Much of what is wrong in our world today—the inhumanity, inequalities and injustices—stem from lack of caring love. But to claim, as the songwriter did, that 'all the world needs is love, sweet love,' is to overstate the case.

Love must go hand in hand with an understanding of the situation to which love has to be applied. If separated from truth, love can hurt rather than heal, smother rather than mother.

Parents must learn the right and wrong ways of expressing love. Parental love needs to be supplemented by parental intelligence.

Likewise those who work and counsel in our hospitals, churches, schools and advice centres must undergo lengthy periods of training—for love without truth can easily degenerate into mistaken kindness or cosy sentimentality.

Loving people does not always involve giving them what they want, or always agreeing with them—Christian love requires not only the caring heart, but the thinking mind. It requires sensitivity, and an understanding of what ennobles life and what degrades it.

The Church speaks of Jesus as 'The Truth,' because she believes that at one point in history, and in one person —a Man from Nazareth—the truth about the nature of God, and the meaning and purpose of life, was more clearly revealed than at any other time.

Like the Jewish prophets before him, one of Jesus' main objectives was to correct the unworthy beliefs which many of his contemporaries had of God and what God required of them.

Jesus was well aware how wrong beliefs can quickly become the parents of scores of wrong actions. Think of how Adolf Hitler's substitution of belief in the German Fatherland for God the Father—the Führer for Jesus and the spirit of German nationalism for the Holy Spirit —plunged the world into a war that cost millions of lives.

One of the aims of my own ministry is to try and purge Christian belief of superstition and unworthy concepts of God: the idea that God is more concerned about what we don't do on Sundays than what we do the rest of the week, that God loves Protestants and white people more than Roman Catholics and black people, that God loves only 'born-again' Christians.

These ideas are, I believe, incompatible with the truth of the Gospel. Part of the burden of preaching week by week is trying to make sure you get it right.

My desire to share with others what I believe to be the truth of the Gospel, springs not from intolerance of other people's beliefs, but from a deep conviction that there is no other religion that fills the words *God, man* and *woman* with such fullness of meaning, or that so illuminates and enriches life as the Christian faith does.

Most people in their saner moments acknowledge that the picture Jesus painted of God in his parable of the prodigal son is unsurpassed in the world's religious literature; and that Christ's way—of reconciling rather than dividing, serving rather than dominating, forgiving rather than avenging, being prayerful rather than anxious, humble rather than proud, loving rather than hating—is a better way than the world's way. Paul could say with justification, 'Now I will show you the best way of all.'

Truth is important, but if not spoken in love it can be unbalanced and offensive. It can leave deep wounds and divide husband from wife, parent from child, employer from employee. Candour must go hand in hand with courtesy.

The kind of dogmatic orthodoxy which wants to have its version of the truth imposed on all has resulted in warring sects, bitter controversies, persecutions and sometimes even massacres. One recalls the fierce condemnation of Galileo by a loveless Church, for teaching that the earth revolves round the sun; and of Michael Servetus for teaching that the blood circulates in our bodies.

When a concern for orthodoxy is divorced from love, the results are still nightmarish. One thinks of the fear instilled, and suffering caused, by extreme Islamic fundamentalists—Koran in one hand, Kalashnikov rifle in the other.

One thinks also of bigoted, loveless church men and women, sometimes more concerned with sniffing out heresy and denouncing other denominations than helping human need. A few seem to have a limitless capacity for disapproval. In fact I can think of people who had more grace as pagans, than as Pharisees.

Christianity with caring, forgiving love at the very heart

of it greatly enriches life. (This love was so wonderfully exhibited by Mr Wilson of Enniskillen whose daughter Marie was killed in a bomb explosion). On the other hand loveless sectarian Christianity, as exhibited by others in Northern Ireland, often brings out the very worst in people.

The Church can survive without buildings and ministers, but it cannot survive without a profound concern for the truth of the Gospel and belief in the healing power of Christian love.

Truth and *love* were found in perfect harmony in Jesus of Nazareth: 'I am come,' said Jesus to Pilate, 'to bear witness to the truth.' Jesus' concern for truth was equalled only by his thoughtful compassion. It is a tragedy that some of his followers have settled for either one or the other. For when truth and caring love are separated, the salt loses its saltness.